"In this intrigu
the numerous
especially in th
remove those 'stones' in our lives that prevent us from entering
more deeply into the Easter mystery of Christ. An adept New
Testament scholar and a poetic spiritual writer, she provides us
with a fresh way of hearing texts we too easily overlook. If you
are seeking spiritual nourishment, especially during Lent, this
is the right book for you."

—Frank J. Matera, professor emeritus, The Catholic
University of America

"Bonnie Thurston writes with the skill of a biblical scholar and
the soul of one who has spent hours in silence before the text.
Her latest book exemplifies this. She invites us into the text of
Luke's Gospel, and the text of Jesus' life as he enters his final
days in Jerusalem. In doing this we are asked to look within at
the text of our own lives to find and recognize the stones we
have carried that need to be rolled away in order for Easter to
occur in us. The 'stones' unearthed in this book will provide
nourishment on the journey to Easter."

—Mary Coloe, University of Divinity Melbourne

"This winsome and wise book quickly engages the reader's
imagination. By directing attention to the things that are
needful, Thurston's deeply personal yet exegetically informed
meditations are guaranteed to provoke serious reflection."

—Dale C. Allison, Jr., Princeton Theological Seminary

"Bonnie Thurston's book *The Stones of the Last Week* is a wonderful series of poetic meditations suitable for the journey toward Easter. Fortified by solid biblical exegesis, the author wends her narrative around the rocks and stones of the Gospel narrative with subtle panache. A great right-brain supplement to the standard treatments, and an exemplary guide in learning the art of drawing life from the Scriptures."

—Michael Casey, OCSO, author of *The Longest Psalm*

"Bonnie Thurston furnishes us with a modern example of patristic interpretation in which every passage and word of Scripture bears spiritual meaning. Drawing on necessary historical-critical scholarship, she builds a whole matrix of geological, cultural, and metaphorical views of rocks and stones and incorporates them into the context of Christ's passion, death, and resurrection. The result is an exegetically sound and scripturally rich analysis of Scripture set within the human condition now bathed in the saving grace of Christ."

—Michael Patella, OSB, Saint John's School of Theology and Seminary

"With her characteristic poetic flare and deep spiritual insight, Bonnie Thurston leads readers into a profound encounter with Christ through the rocks and stones that strew his path in his last week of earthly life. Especially helpful during Lent, this little gem of a book is one I will return to again and again."

—Barbara E. Reid, OP, president and Carroll Stuhlmueller, CP, Distinguished Professor of New Testament Studies, Catholic Theological Union, Chicago

The Stones of the Last Week

Impediments to Easter

Bonnie B. Thurston

LITURGICAL PRESS
Collegeville, Minnesota

litpress.org

Cover art: detail from a drawing, design for a stained glass window, ca. 1909–12, Izabel. M. Coles. Public domain.

Library of Congress Cataloging-in-Publication Data

Names: Thurston, Bonnie Bowman, author.
Title: The stones of the last week : impediments to Easter / Bonnie B.
    Thurston.
Description: Collegeville, MN : Liturgical Press, [2024] | Summary:
    "In The Stones of the Last Week, Bonnie B. Thurston reflects
    on the Passion narratives in Luke 19-24, and explores the many
    references to stones, both literal and spiritual, that impeded Jesus's
    last week with a view to their significance for our own journey"—
    Provided by publisher.
Identifiers: LCCN 2024008786 (print) | LCCN 2024008787 (ebook)
    | ISBN 9780814669457 (trade paperback) | ISBN 9780814669464
    (epub) | ISBN 9780814688946 (pdf)
Subjects: LCSH: Bible. Luke—Criticism, interpretation, etc. | Bible.
    Acts—Criticism, interpretation, etc. | Easter. | BISAC: RELIGION
    / Biblical Meditations / New Testament | RELIGION / Holidays /
    Easter & Lent
Classification: LCC BS2595.2 .T487 2024 (print) | LCC BS2595.2
    (ebook) | DDC 226.4/06—dc23/eng/20240617
LC record available at https://lccn.loc.gov/2024008786
LC ebook record available at https://lccn.loc.gov/2024008787

For my brother

"Look to the rock from which you were hewn,
and to the quarry from which you were dug."

Isaiah 51:1b

Contents

Acknowledgments and Thanksgivings

Stones of the Last Week had its inception in 2015 when the Episcopal churches of Wheeling and Moundsville, West Virginia, gathered for a Wednesday evening Lenten study at St. Matthew's Church in Wheeling. Fr. Mark Seitz, then rector of St. Matthew's, invited me to give the talks. I had recently noticed how many "rocks" there are in Luke 19:28–24:53 and so built a Lenten series around that theme. This accounts for the book's conversation tone and diction. I am grateful for that invitation and for those who attended the talks and asked such thoughtful questions. The group effort facilitated a more nuanced and helpful book.

Gratitude continues to St. Matthew's. Its clergy, staff, and fellow parishioners provide good worship, good fellowship, and a challenging presence. I am also thankful for the Christian Church (Disciples of Christ) parishes in which I was raised and educated, and in which it has been my privilege to serve as a teacher, preacher, and occasional interim pastor.

Nobody writes a book alone, and one certainly is never published without the help of many people. I have had a happy relationship with Liturgical Press for over twenty years. (I hope it has been happy for them.) Their kindness, patience, and helpfulness are legion. Thanks to Br. Aelred Senna, OSB, for his advocacy of the manuscript. Continuing gratitude to Hans Christoffersen, editorial director (who also facilitates new culinary experiences); Stephanie Lancour, production editor (who assists with such lovely volumes); and Michelle Verkuilen, associate marketing director (who gets the word out). Each has remarkable patience of which I am the beneficiary.

Special thanks to Paraclete Press for permission to reprint the poems "Precious Rocks" and "The Stone" from my *Practicing Silence: New and Selected Verses*[1] and to the Abbey of Gethsemani and New Directions Publishing for permission to close this book with a quotation from Thomas Merton's poem "In Silence."[2] I am a pedant and work hard not to do so, but if I have inadvertently omitted a citation I would be grateful to have it brought to my attention and will correct my omission in any future printings of the book.

1. *Practicing Silence: New and Selected Verses* by Bonnie Thurston. Copyright 2014 by Bonnie Thurston. Used by permission of Paraclete Press. www.paracletepress.com.

2. "In Silence," by Thomas Merton, from *The Collected Poems of Thomas Merton*, copyright ©1957 by The Abbey of Gethsemani. Reprinted by permission of New Directions Publishing Corp.

I am blessed by a group of attentive, smart, challenging, and wonderfully fun-to-be-with friends. Many thanks to them. They know who they are.

Finally, this small book is a reflection on the last week of Jesus' life as recorded in Luke's gospel. I hope it makes a good Lenten companion; however, it's not strictly a "Lenten book." The "stones" herein represent the impediments, the obstacles, to the fullness of life that the resurrection of the Lord Jesus initiated and offers. I hope it will help you remove some of your "stones." Writing the book helped me dispose of some of mine.

Bonnie Thurston
The Anchorage
Wheeling, West Virginia

Introduction

Reading carefully through the last week of Jesus in Luke 19:28–24:11, I noticed that it was littered with stones. There are many significant references to stones in Luke's text. (For a list, see page 12.) This realization put me in mind of the beloved African American hymn by the poet James Weldon Johnson, "Lift Every Voice and Sing," which contains the line "Stony the road we trod."[1] Stony the road Jesus trod in his last week. It was full of impediments. The Latin root of the word is *ped*, "foot," what trips over stones. Impediments are things that hinder, impede, or stand between what one wishes to reach or accomplish and that goal. As we read through Luke's gospel account, the stones we encounter in the company of Jesus challenge us to consider our own impediments and help us to prepare for his crucifixion, resurrection, and the new life they offer.

This might be a good Lenten book for a busy person in that it provides one chapter per week of Lent. But it is an

---

1. James Weldon Johnson, 1921 (public domain).

appropriate study at any time of year. Without questioning the historicity of Luke's narrative, I ask the reader to assume a certain non-literal or metaphorical cast of mind. That is to say, the stones we encounter in Luke's text are (mostly) *real* stones. You wouldn't want to stub a toe against one. But they are also metaphors for difficulties, hindrances, or obstructions in the spiritual life. The first chapter, based on 1 Peter 2:4-8, introduces the idea of impediments and living stones. It is followed by chapters that explore the stones in Luke's text: talking stones, stones of destruction, impermanent stones, stones that measure distances, and a single stone that marks both death and life.

Although it reflects serious New Testament scholarship, this is not a scholarly book on Luke. But it might enhance your reading to know a bit about the evangelist Luke and his first audience. If this doesn't interest you, you may skip to chapter one, but I hope you won't.[2]

As is true with all four evangelists, we don't know a lot about Luke personally. The Muratorian Canon, written in Rome around AD 170, suggests Luke was a Syrian from Antioch, a physician who accompanied Paul on his journeys,

---

2. For more background information on Luke's gospel from several theological perspectives, see the entry on Luke's gospel by Darrell L. Bock in *Dictionary of Jesus and the Gospels* (Leicester, England: InterVarsity Press, 1992), Raymond E. Brown, *An Introduction to the New Testament* (New York: Doubleday, 1997), and Luke Timothy Johnson, *The Gospel of Luke*, Sacra Pagina (Collegeville, MN: Liturgical Press, 1991).

who remained unmarried, and died at the age of eighty-four in Boeotia in central Greece. There is no independent confirmation of any of this. There are three references in Pauline writings to *a* Luke (Phlm 24; Col 4:10-14; 2 Tim 4:11), but he may or not be the evangelist. What a close reading of the text of Luke reveals is that its author was someone with a Hellenistic education who wrote excellent (often beautiful) Greek, had wide knowledge of the Torah and Hebrew Scripture, and was a first-rate storyteller.

Perhaps the only Gentile evangelist, Luke, through his authorship of both the gospel and the Acts of the Apostles, is responsible for about 27 percent of the New Testament. His gospel belongs to the middle period of first century AD gospel writing, after the composition of Mark (65–70) and before John (95–110). Since Luke 21:20 may be a reference to the siege of Jerusalem in the Jewish War of AD 66–70, a date in the 80s, perhaps 85, is likely and accounts for Luke's dependence on Mark and the material he shares with Matthew. No ancient tradition names the provenance of Luke's gospel, although southern Greece has been suggested, a place outside Roman Palestine where there would be Greek speakers who knew Hebrew scriptural traditions.

Luke's gospel was consciously shaped for Greek-speaking readers. It omits "foreign" (non-Greek) words and corrects Mark's grammar and improves his style. It skillfully uses literary conventions of the Greco-Roman world, contains a literary prologue, seems to know biographies of Hellenistic philosophers, and employs a journey motif much beloved of Jews, Greeks, and Romans. Francis J. Moloney notes that "an important theme of the Gospel of Luke and its companion work . . . is the theme of the journey." The "journey leads to Jerusalem, where the paschal events take place."[3] Luke's rhythms and patterns are those of the Septuagint (Hebrew Scripture in Greek), which also reflects not only the Jewish backgrounds of Jesus and his first followers but a Greek fondness for "archaizing."

Luke may be the first early Christian to understand that the *parousia*, the return of Jesus, would be delayed. After the destruction of the Temple, the geographical center of gravity for Christianity was shifting to Rome. If Jesus were to return immediately, Christians could revile the Roman Empire and await its destruction. If the return of Jesus were delayed, then Christians must come to terms with the empire, learn to live and evangelize within it. For Christianity to be sustained and spread, for Jesus' life and teaching to be preserved, a new kind of literary approach was required, something to appeal to the tastes of educated Greeks and Romans who might find Christianity objectionable for at least three reasons.

First, its origins were among the Jews, almost universally disliked and the largest minority group in the empire. So Luke depicts Christianity as universal in scope as God's

3. Francis J. Moloney, SDB, *The Resurrection of the Messiah: A Narrative Commentary on the Resurrection Accounts in the Four Gospels* (New York: Paulist, 2013), 79.

promises to Israel are extended to Gentiles. Second, in a
world that thought old was better (imagine!), Christianity
was a "newfangled" teaching. So Luke shows how it fulfills
ancient purposes of God. Third, it might be politically dangerous (Nero attacked it). To say "Jesus is Lord" implied
Caesar wasn't. So Luke downplays "revolutionary" aspects
of Christianity. In Luke's gospel, Pilate declares Jesus innocent three times. In Acts, Rome protects Christianity.
Luke's gospel is the first great Christian apologia, a work
written to take into consideration and answer the doubts,
difficulties, and objections about it. While preserving its
Jewish character and origins, Luke strives to commend
Christianity to those outside Judaism, to demonstrate that
the church and state can live together. This is no small task,
but it is the genius of Luke to use history in the service of
theology and for pastoral purposes.

As do all three synoptic gospels, Luke's narrative moves
inexorably toward Jerusalem: "He took the twelve aside and
said to them, 'See, we are going up to Jerusalem'" (18:31).
There prophecy will be fulfilled, and the Son of Man will be
killed and rise again. "But they understood nothing about
all these things" (18:34). Passing through Jericho, which is
on the main road from Galilee to Jerusalem, Jesus encoun-
ters Zacchaeus (19:1-10), then tells "a parable, because he
was near Jerusalem" (19:11). And "after he had said this,
he went on ahead, going up to Jerusalem" (19:28). The city
is up the mountain from Jericho. Jesus leads. Disciples follow. They approach Bethphage and Bethany (19:29; again,

geographical accuracy), where the disciples commandeer a colt, and Jesus' descent into death begins as he rides "down from the Mount of Olives" (19:37) into Jerusalem to the acclamation of the disciples and the criticism of others, to whom Jesus says, "I tell you, if these were silent, the *stones* would shout out" (19:37-40, italics mine). And there the stones of our exploration commence.

I agree in essence with Rowan Williams that "Christians read the Bible not as a document from history but as a world into which they enter so that God may meet them."[4] Thus, I have kept three interpretive principles in mind as I have thought about the stones of Jesus' last week. First, I have tried to be faithful to what the text of Luke actually writes, though I do push the boundaries in the excursus and chapter 4. Second, I presume that religious language, and especially that of the gospels, is multivalent, that is, it has multiple levels of meaning. For example, Lukan texts relate historical events in the life of Jesus, and the elements of those events can also have symbolic or metaphorical meanings. Thus, third, we can read Luke's gospel on several levels: that of the narrative of the life of Jesus, that of what it reveals to us about Luke's original audience, and that of its meaning in our own day. These three principles require a certain intellectual agility on the part of the reader with

---

4. Rowan Williams, *God with Us: The Meaning of the Cross and Resurrection—Then and Now* (London: SPCK, 2017), 87.

whom the writer hopes to share insights into the enduring spiritual meanings and realities in the text.

While some are boulders and some are pebbles, we all face impediments, difficulties, blockages to the fullness of life Jesus offers. It is my hope that considering some of the stones of Jesus' last week may help us to negotiate the things that trip us up as we, too, move toward death and resurrection, and in that universal process learn not to "look for the living among the dead" (Luke 24:5) but to "look to the rock from which you were hewn, / and to the quarry from which you were dug" (Isa 51:1b).

CHAPTER ONE

Impediments and Living Stones

(1 Peter 2:4-8)

Why are we thinking about rocks?

Why are we thinking about *rocks*? If you can bear with a little bit of meandering, I'll try to explain. I am told by those who dabble in astrology (I am most assuredly not one) that the twelve signs of the Zodiac are divided into four elements: earth, air, fire, and water. I don't know which one rules my sign, but it might be earth, because I am so taken by rocks. Those who have been in my home know that the windowsills tend to be cluttered with stones and that one used to have to shove a large, doorstop rock out of the way to get into the bathroom. (It's an old house; the doors are out of alignment.) I have picked up rocks in various places that have moved, delighted, or distressed me, and carried them home as small souvenirs. They are precious rocks, a phrase I used to title this poem that I wrote some time ago.

"Precious Rocks"

*"I will give a white stone, and on the white stone
    is written a new name that no one knows
    except the one who receives it." (Rev 2:17)*

Perhaps this is why
I have always been
a collector of stones,
lined dusty window sills
of home, retreat house,
vacation cabin
with small impediments
of meandering journeys:

a tiny, purple chip
from Sinai's height;

Wyoming soapstone
smeared with copper ore;
deceptively flecked schist
full of fools' gold;

once, in Virginia,
where rock is red
with ferrous oxide,
a three inch obelisk

of gray granite
fused to milk quartz;

Iona's green marble,
the crimson pebbles
of its martyrs' beach;

(my perennial favorite)
a water worn smooth
white palm sized stone.

The hand luggage
of my travels
is heavy with them,
the basement littered
with petrified souvenirs
from forgotten places.

Reader, do not chuckle
in bemused indulgence.
"Stony the road I trod."
On life's rocky road,
it is serious business,
to search the hard,
animate beauty of stone
for one's own hidden
and secret name.[1]

---

1. Bonnie Thurston, "Precious Rocks," in Thurston, *Practicing Silence: New and Selected Verses* (Brewster, MA: Paraclete, 2014), 62–63.

Somehow, these stones embody the energy of places and are thus, in their inert way, alive. This is not a "witchy" way of thinking. The New Testament itself speaks of "living stones." More on that in a moment.

It might be this rock obsession that led me to notice how many rocks and stones there are in the last week of our Lord's life as St. Luke records it in 19:28 through 24:53. The following is a fairly complete list:

19:40	stones that shout out
19:44	not one stone left on another
20:6	people who cast stones
20:17	stones builders reject and cornerstones
21:5	beautiful stones
21:6	not one stone left on another (again)
22:41	a stone's throw away
23:53	a rock-hewn tomb
24:2	the stone rolled away

Some of these stones are literal. Some of them are metaphors in Jesus' last teachings. Some of them are both. All of them are alive with significance on the journey of Jesus to his crucifixion and resurrection. Some of them suggest difficult things for us to take on board, things that might stand in our way, *skandalon* (literally "that which causes stumbling"), as we make the journey to Easter. The word *impediment* came to my mind, probably because its Latin root, *impedire* ("entangle" or "hamper"), originally had to do with the feet (root word, *ped*). Impediments trip us up on our journeys. In legal language, an impediment is a bar (usually blood or affinity) that, for example, prevents a marriage. Impediments can prevent us from getting to Easter, the cosmic wedding feast of the lamb.

Most generally, an impediment is what stands between us and our goal. My theological conviction is that the important goal of the Christian life is Easter and "eastering," both a noun (something basically static, a first-century event) and a verb (something active, the process of reaching something). I mean that in several senses.

First, the whole liturgical year beginning at Advent moves toward Easter: from human, temporal life to, well, we don't know exactly what *form*, but certainly eternal life. Second, Easter is the goal of the life of Jesus, although I rather doubt that he had it or that word in mind as he trudged down the Jordan River Valley trying to sort out what discipleship meant for his not exactly brilliant little community of Galilean men and women followers. (For the women, see Mark 15:40-41 and Luke 8:1-3.) This journey includes one of Luke's two special sections or insertions, 9:51–18:15, material he inserted in the narrative order given by St. Mark. Easter is the crown of Christology. Jesus is crucified and raised from the dead by God, and that raising is God's seal of approval on the Beloved, his obedience, teaching, and life. One way to say this is to say that the Easter event elevated Jesus of Nazareth or, if you follow the Christ hymns in Paul (Phil 2:6-11 and Col 1:15-20), *returned* Jesus of Nazareth to his status as the cosmic, reigning, eternal Christ.

Third, the raising of Jesus as "firstborn from the dead" (Col 1:18) has critical implications for Christians, personally. The word *firstborn* isn't used to describe a child unless there are other children in the family. And there are other siblings in Christ's family. They are us. As the Pauline letters frequent use of the word *heir* suggests (see, for example, Gal 3:28-29, 4:1ff, or Rom 8:17), we're God's other children, given a share in God's life through Jesus *and* (this is where the rubber hits the road for most of us) promised that we, too, will be raised from death to life. This promise is the source of a Christian's hope.

But Easter is more than an event in the history of the first century of the Common Era, more than something that has happened to Jesus and will happen to us. Easter is an ongoing process of life-giving and growth. As previously suggested, *Easter* is a noun *and* a verb. The great English poet, Fr. Gerard Manley Hopkins, SJ, uses *Easter* as a verb in just the sense I mean. He invites Jesus to "Easter" in people, and he speaks of "eastering" as the process of bringing life from death. The last stanza of his great poem "The Wreck of the Deutschland" has these lines: "Let him easter in us, be a dayspring to the dimness of us, / be a crimson-cresseted east."[2] The season of Lent, for example, helps us to focus on

2. Gerard Manley Hopkins, *The Poems of Gerard Manley Hopkins*, ed. W. H. Gardner and N. H. MacKenzie (Oxford: Oxford University Press, 1967–70), 63.

the goal of Easter as an event of past and future. But in a wider sense, Jesus invites us to participate in the process of eastering, of moving from what is dead in ourselves to what is living, to live into the promise inherent in what John's Jesus believed was his raison d'être: "I came that they may have life, and have it abundantly" (John 10:10).

The problem is that there are impediments between us and both Easter and eastering. Now, perhaps, you see where I'm going with this rock business. Impediments are what stand between us and our goals, between where we are and where we'd like to be, between us and new life. As I reflected on impediments, I noticed that, even though these aren't the only categories, and they, in fact, can overlap, impediments seem to be of two primary types: external and internal.

The external impediments might be called "circumstantial," the things in life that seem to block us from our goals. They are what Shakespeare calls "the slings and arrows that flesh is heir to." You will have noticed that life isn't perfect and that some of us start out with a great many more impediments than others. Some of us are born with a few stones in our pockets, and some of us are born with millstones around our necks. I don't know why this is, only that it is. Some of us face more challenges in life than others of us do and must muster more courage and wisdom and strength and sometimes get more help than others of us. But everybody has external impediments of some sort. It is the human condition. If you don't think you have any circumstantial impediments, you are in more trouble than the folks who know they do.

There is also, perhaps, a sort of "intermediate" impediment that is halfway between external and internal. I tend to think of them in terms of cultural conditioning, the "should's" and "ought's" and "have to's" that come because we were born into a certain race, culture, socioeconomic class, religious tradition, and country (or subculture within a country). I think, for example, that the impediment of acquisitiveness and of hoarding stuff is an external impediment internalized. We take in the "buy stuff" message that makes capitalism work almost before it becomes a matter of choice. But it *is* a matter of choice, as are many of the imposed-from-outside expectations that imprison many folks. It is possible, for example, to choose whether you want to live from an abundance or a scarcity model, to live as if there is enough for everybody rather than as if there isn't enough to go around, whether you want to live the "more is better" rather than "enough is enough" or the "less is better if it means others can have enough" model.

Internal impediments are both easier and dicier to deal with. Things inside us can keep us from reaching the goals, the life, the Easter set before us. Internal stones can slow or block our way to Easter. The good news in this rather glum pronouncement is that we might have more control than we have chosen to exert over the internal impediments than the external ones. Granted, internal impediments can be externally caused. We can inherit predispositions to certain diseases, dispositions, or attitudes. Or we can be treated wretchedly as children, so wretchedly that our interior life is warped, our interior lights are extinguished. I don't think I need to give many examples or go deeply into this. You know what I mean. It is possible to overcome internal impediments, but one must be very courageous and frequently have help to recover and relight our interior lamps.

The internal impediment I have in mind as a detriment to eastering is the sort of rock we put in our own path. Often we aren't conscious of our self-generated impediments, and it is critical to awaken to them. For example, our own attitudes can be impediments. We can have taken in the prejudices of our parents or the narrowness or xenophobia of our community or culture. We can continually make unexamined or poor choices with regard to mental and physical health. We can decide that, in response to the external impediments of our lives, we'll be just plain old "cussed," dishing out more nastiness than we received. We can give in to our predispositions, depression, judgmentalism or . . . you fill in the blank with your own internal impediments. But we also have the choice to make, and we can begin the work of making, our internal rough places smooth, or at least smoother (see Isa 40:3-4). We can choose the internal equivalent of a shovel and a rake and maybe even a pickax. We might even need to call in a front loader to start digging out the stones that stand between us and both Easter and eastering.

This process is a divine invitation to us. It presumes that Easter is our goal, that we desire eastering in our lives. It presumes that we desire to be fully alive. I remind you that Trappist writer Thomas Merton wrote, "Your life is shaped by the end you live for. You are made in the image of what you desire."[3] Eastering, a fuller, more vibrant life, is about putting down the stones we carry unnecessarily or removing the impediments that stand between us and what we desire. It is about examining the ends that we live for. We'll come back to the idea of putting down stones in a later chapter. I have one more idea to share now, and it is a paradox: the journey to Easter is to approach the Living Stone so that *we* can become living stones. We set aside our stones to become one!

Sometime between AD 60 and 90 (about a generation after Jesus was raised from the dead), someone, perhaps the apostle Peter, wrote a letter to the Christians in Asia Minor. Christians were a minority and, like our brethren in the Coptic Church in Egypt and the Orthodox Christians in Syria and Turkey today, not a protected one. Increasingly Gentiles were becoming Christians, and in those days you wouldn't want your sister to marry one. Christianity had begun to make inroads into the hierarchical and patriarchal cultures to *change* them. So the author of this letter writes, first, to encourage the Christians by reminding them of what and in Whom they believe and, secondarily, to suggest they are good citizens and share some values with the wider culture. In the midst of an exhortation Peter writes

3. Thomas Merton, *Thoughts in Solitude* (New York: Farrar, Straus and Giroux: 1965), 56.

the following: "Come to him, a living stone, though rejected by mortals yet chosen and precious in God's sight, and like living stones, let yourself be built into a spiritual house, to be a holy priesthood, to offer spiritual sacrifices acceptable to God through Jesus Christ" (1 Pet 2:4-5).

Then the writer of 1 Peter quotes Isaiah 28:16 about the chosen and precious cornerstone in Zion—"See, I am laying in Zion a foundation stone, / a tested stone, / a precious cornerstone, a sure foundation"—and also Psalm 118:22 with its outrageous assertion that "[t]he stone that the builders rejected / has become the chief cornerstone."

First Peter 2:4-8a sets out themes and quotes texts that we will be exploring in future chapters. It invites us to come to Christ the "living stone," the thing that seems dead but is alive. The writer has several Hebrew scriptural ideas in mind, perhaps most dramatically the water from the rock in the Exodus account. (More on that later in an excursus.) The text issues an extraordinary invitation: "like living stones, let *yourselves* be built into a spiritual house" (italics mine). We are to clear out our impediments to Easter so that we can become the "living stones" in a spiritual house someone else is building. Odd, but there it is. This might be the New Testament equivalent of the Hebrew Bible's image of being clay in the potter's hands. (See Isa 64:8 and Jer 18:6.)

We, you and I, are intended to be the building materials of a house for God and for others. Building materials give themselves over to the builder to be used as he or she chooses. This requires passivity and detachment that are

very difficult for most Western people. We want to draw
the blueprints for the building or do the interior decoration
rather than be the materials someone else uses. But Jesus
Christ is the cornerstone of this building. Rejected by some
people, Christ the rock is chosen by and precious to God
and to believers. He has become "the head of the corner"
to believers but a stone that makes others "stumble" (as we
noted, the word in Greek is *skandalon*, from which we get
"scandal") "and a rock that makes them fall" (1 Pet 2:8). In
short, an impediment. Stranger and stranger.

We will be working through some of this strangeness in
the chapters that follow. For the moment, let me summarize
and then suggest two optional bits of "homework" to be
done now before you go on to the next chapter. I am using
"stone" as a metaphor or shorthand for "impediments,"
which are the things that stand between us and Easter,
which I take to be both an event in history—a noun—and
a process of life-giving and life-bringing—a verb. The passages in Luke 19:28 through 24:53 that mention "stones"
will illuminate what some of those impediments might be
for us and how we might go about removing them. Very
simply, I am inviting us to consider what stands between
us and the fullness of life Jesus came to give us and to get
rid of as many of those "stones" as possible. The ultimate
goal of the process is not just our personal well-being, ful-
fillment, and eternal life (this last we are already have by
virtue of our baptism). It is that we *become* "living stones,"
sources of security and life-giving for others. We are to

become Easter people in order to share our fullness of life in Christ with others.

For Prayer and Pondering

I suggest we begin with two exercises in "giving up," neither easy, but the first perhaps more obvious than the second.

Suggestion #1. Make a list of your impediments to Easter and eastering. You might want to make two lists, actually: a list of the external impediments and a list of the internal ones. Then, when you know what the "barriers" are, think about and, more importantly, pray about what you can do to remove some of them. Ask the Lord to show you what stands in the way of the fullness of life he wants to give you and how to go about removing the obstacles that you can remove. Strategize a bit about it. Do you want to start with the little ones and work up to the big ones, or go after the boulders first and then sweep away the pebbles? The point is to become aware of what is "in the way" of Easter/life and make some concrete (!) plans for action to clear out some rubble. In spite of the work, it will be sort of fun to scratch things off your "to do" list.

Suggestion #2. This is harder, and you may want to approach it in different ways. Make a list of six things that make your life worth living. Or list your six most cherished things. I won't define or circumscribe whether "things" for you might be material, spiritual, attitudes, ideas, convictions, possessions, or persons. That's for you to decide. Here's the hard part: mentally "give up" the most expendable of the six. (Yes, I know. It's hard.) Thereafter, "give up" the next most expendable item. Of the six what would be the most expendable? And then, of the five that are left, what is most expendable, and so on until you are left with one. This one will be what the theologian Paul Tillich called your "ultimate concern." It will tell you a great deal about who you are. Remember that Thomas Merton says you're made in the image of what you desire![4] And mostly, unless we are fully realized Buddhists, we cling to what we desire. This exercise will also give you insight into what Easter/eastering, greater life, the fullness of life, might mean for you.

4. For more on this, see Bonnie B. Thurston, *Shaped by the End You Live For: Thomas Merton's Monastic Spirituality* (Collegeville, MN: Liturgical Press, 2020).

CHAPTER TWO

Shouting Stones
and Scattered Stones

(Luke 19:40-41 & 21:5-6)

Facing life's challenges.

Impediments to Easter/eastering are the things that stand between us and resurrection life. In this chapter we shall begin to examine some of the particular stones (actual and metaphorical) encountered in the last week of Jesus' life as St. Luke records it: the shouting stones and the scattered stones.

Shouting Stones

"I tell you if these were silent, the stones would shout out."
(Luke 19:40)

These words of Jesus occur toward the end of Luke's extended account of Jesus' "triumphal entry" into Jerusalem (19:28-48). Some Lukan details of that event are of interest. After Jesus calls Zacchaeus in Jericho and tells a parable about fig trees, Luke comments, "After he had said this, he went on ahead, going up to Jerusalem" (19:28). Luke makes it clear that Jesus leads and disciples follow. In fact, as noted in the introduction, one does go "up" from Jericho, the oasis city in the Jordan Valley, to Jerusalem on Mount Zion. Going uphill involves exertion.

Luke is interested in the geographical progression of the day. Jesus goes "up to Jerusalem" (19:28). The route from Jericho would, indeed, pass through "Bethphage and Bethany at the place called the Mount of Olives" (19:29) and move through them to "the path down from the Mount of Olives" (19:37), from which one has a spectacular view of the city. Thus the geography is correct when Luke notes that Jesus "saw the city, he wept over it" (19:41) before "he entered the temple" (19:45). It is at the apex of the path with its vista of Jerusalem, before it drops down toward the Kidron Valley, that "the whole multitude of disciples began to praise God" (19:37) and chant an acclamation. Metaphorically, Jesus' "descent" will continue to his crucifixion.

At this point "some of the Pharisees in the crowd"— What are they doing there? Are they Jesus' disciples? Spying on Jesus?—order Jesus to stop the ruckus (19:38), especially since the acclamation from Psalm 118:26 calls Jesus a "king" (Luke 19:38). In the fraught political atmosphere of Passover, a feast that celebrates the liberation of Israel from slavery and was so dangerous in the first century that the Roman governor came from his seaside villa at Caesarea Maritima with his army to be resident in Jerusalem. The acclamation is an act of sedition if ever there were one. Jesus says that if the disciples were silent, "the stones"—of which, you may trust me, there are plenty in that locale—"would shout out" (literally, "the stones will cry out" [19:40]). I suspect the Pharisees would have recognized that here Jesus alludes to the prophet Habakkuk who in the course of a woe oracle suggests that buildings, themselves, will cry out against injustice: "The very stones will cry out from the wall" (Hab 2:11). As in 1 Peter 1, here the stones are "living"; they would cry out for the coming king of justice.

The operative surprise in Luke's text, and undoubtedly for us, is that nobody expects *stones* to speak. They are inert matter, dense, and dumb. Or so the physics many of us learned in school suggested. But the Seraphic Hymn has always been correct: "Heaven and earth are full of [God's] glory." Now theoretical physics (which often sounds a lot like theology) is suggesting that *nothing* is "inert," that everything pulses with energy. For example, "glory" is traditionally depicted by "light," a form of energy, movement.

But these are matters for another time. The point here is that the very stones would acclaim the one who comes to effect their redemption, because it's not just humans whom Jesus comes to redeem, but every created thing. Paul reminded the Romans that God had always "been understood and seen through the things he has made" (Rom 1:20) and that very creation "waits with eager longing for the revealing of the children of God" (Rom 8:19). Paul's is a cosmic vision of resurrection: "[T]he creation itself will be set free from its bondage to decay and will obtain the freedom of the glory of the children of God. We know that the whole creation has been groaning in labor pains until now; and not only the creation, but we ourselves" (Rom 8:21-22). Not just human beings but everything cries out for redemption and resurrection. And everything is included in God's plan for resurrection, because from the beginning all creation has been part of that plan. Creation was made for resurrection. As Maria Boulding writes, "The resurrection is not simply an event for Jesus personally. It is God's mighty act of salvation and re-creation for the whole cosmos."[1]

On our journey to resurrection, the stones of which Jesus speaks to the Pharisees suggest to us at least three things. First, "shouting" or "crying" stones remind us to think of the implications of Easter in greater than human terms. Although it is certainly about human salvation and eternal life, it is about something "way bigger" than the human or even the planetary. This is not just the insight of more recent theologians like Teilhard de Chardin or Elia Delio. As is clear from the letter to the Romans, the apostle Paul, a contemporary of Jesus of Nazareth, glimpsed it not

1. Maria Boulding, OSB, *Gateway to Resurrection* (London: Burns & Oates, 2010), 126.

long after the historical event of the resurrection of Jesus. Paul, or perhaps one of his disciples, wrote confidently at the outset of Ephesians that God "has made known to us the mystery of his will . . . a plan for the fullness of time, to gather up all things in [Christ], *things in heaven and things on earth*" (Eph 1:9-10; italics mine).

Second, the "shouting stones" remind us to listen for messages in unexpected places. Sometimes we don't hear God's voice because God is speaking in places and things and persons to which and to whom we aren't listening. In the Roman letter Paul voiced an insight that has often been echoed by Christian theologians and non-Christian philosophers: God is evident in creation. Pushed to its limit, this idea means that everything that exists speaks God. Yes, *everything*. The problem is often that our listening is too constricted. We decide, or we are taught (alas, sometimes by the church), that God only speaks in certain ways, certain places, through certain people. And so the realm of our listening becomes very narrow. The "shouting stones" suggest that God might well be heard *exactly* where speech seems impossible.

Thomas Merton wrote a poem called "In Silence." It has to do with listening in places where you don't expect speech, in the stones of a wall which speaks your name.[2] Just the

2. "In Silence" plays on just this reality as it asks the reader to "Listen to the stones of the wall." Merton, *The Collected Poems of Thomas Merton* (New York: New Directions, 1977), 280.

place you don't think it's *possible* to "hear your name," to know you are being spoken to, summoned, loved by God, may be the place that is *trying* to speak to you. Did you ever notice that bit about the white stone in the Revelation to John? "I will give a white stone, and on the white stone is written a new name that no one knows except the one who receives it" (Rev 2:17).[3] This is the "new name" promised by Isaiah: "[Y]ou shall be called by a new name / that the mouth of the LORD will give" (Isa 62:2b). But we must listen for it in places we don't expect to hear it.

Third—and this is a bit paradoxical—the silence of stones also speaks because, as the psalmist so frequently asserts, created things praise God by being what they are. "All the earth bows down before you," says the psalmist, "sings to you, sings out your Name" (66:3).[4] Those of us who love birds do so in part because they don't try to be anything but birds; they praise (and reflect) God by doing what birds do.[5] Those of us who love dogs love their dogginess. People to whom I am often drawn are often not the "beautiful people" by society's or our culture's definition but people who are unselfconsciously and completely themselves. Where I come from we call them "characters." Fr. Michael Casey, OCSO, observes that "every saint is an original. There are no stereotypes, no

---

3. See the poem "Precious Rocks" in chapter 1.

4. Translation of *The Book of Common Prayer*, Episcopal Church USA (New York: Church Publishing, 2007), 673.

5. To know more about what birds do, I highly recommend David Allen Sibley's *What It's Like to Be a Bird* (New York: Knopf, 2020).

duplications; each is a unique triumph of divine grace."[6] In part, saints are saints because they don't fight their quirkiness but glorify God by it.

The following story considers stones and speaking from a slightly different but profoundly important point of view. Once in Wales I listened in to a conversation about very, very small churches, mostly those ancient Norman stone churches built in numbers long before modern transportation made many of them slightly redundant. The gentle, old priest who was charged to maintain the liturgy in a number of them spoke, not of the need to increase numbers (though I'm sure he wouldn't oppose that), but of "keeping the prayers going." And then he said, "And if the churches close, the stones will keep the prayer alive." Quite. They pray by being stones and by having absorbed the prayers of centuries. The spiritually attuned and alive "feel" the prayer when they enter such spaces. "Jesus answered the Pharisees, 'I tell you, if these were silent, the stones would shout out'" (Luke 19:40).

Scattered Stones

"[A]nd they will not leave within you one stone upon another." (Luke 19:44)

"[N]ot one stone will be left upon another; all will be thrown down." (Luke 21:6)

6. Michael Casey, OCSO, *Balaam's Donkey: Random Ruminations For Every Day of the Year* (Collegeville, MN: Liturgical Press, 2019), 304.

This same image of "not one stone upon another," an image of absolute destruction, occurs in two melancholy settings in the last week of Jesus. They describe what happens if people don't recognize what the stones know. The first occurrence follows from the last stones we examined, the shouting ones. It is part of the story of Jesus' entry to Jerusalem and one of the most melancholy texts in the gospels. Jesus approaches the city, looks out from the Mount of Olives, and weeps over the place whose name means "peace" but which hasn't done "things that make for peace" (Luke 19:42).

Luke 19:43-44 are of great historical interest to scholars of the gospel. A number of scholars think that Jesus here predicts the siege and destruction of Jerusalem that did, indeed, happen in AD 69–70. If so, these verses are crucial to dating Luke's gospel. The passage harkens back to prophecies and oracles of destruction in the Hebrew Bible. For example, Isaiah declares,

> I [God] will encamp against you;
> I will besiege you with towers
> and raise siegeworks against you. (Isa 29:3)[7]

Additionally, the word *siegeworks* or *ramparts* suggests the siege Jerusalem endured under the Roman general Titus, which did, indeed, result in the complete destruction of the city and of Herod's splendidly restored Temple.

---

7. See also, for example, 2 Kgs 8:11-12; Ps 137:9; Isa 29:3-10, 48:18; Jer 6:6-20; 8:18-21, 15:5, 23:38-40.

"Not one stone upon another" was quite a feat since the historian Josephus wrote that the Herodian stones were 75 feet long and the blocks from which the Temple was constructed were 42 feet in length.[8] So complete was the devastation that the land around the city was sown with salt and the name was changed to the Roman "Aelia Capitolina." Jesus' lament over Jerusalem is reminiscent of his words in Luke 23:27-31 to the "daughters of Jerusalem" even as he was en route to Golgotha and the crucifixion. These almost last words of Jesus, "weep for yourselves and for your children" (23:28), are another prediction of bad times ahead—*big* impediments.

The point in Luke 19:41-44 for our reflection is the fact of the destruction of a city with massive stone walls that were thought to protect people's safety and be impregnable. They weren't. "[T]hey will not leave one stone upon another" (19:44). They didn't. In the narrative, Jesus tries to do something about the problem by "cleansing" the Temple (see Luke 19:45-46).[9] This suggests that there might be some way in which we "living stones" might prevent destruction

8. Quoted in John Wilkinson, *The Jerusalem Jesus Knew: An Archaeological Guide to the Gospels* (Nashville: Thomas Nelson, 1978), 76. And see the section "In the Temple" in the chapter "Jesus Comes to Jerusalem," 70–89.

9. Pace Sr. Mary Coloe whose work on John's gospel repudiates "cleansing" as what was going on. I have twice heard her lecture on this point. Mary L. Coloe, *Dwelling in the Household of God* (Collegeville, MN: Liturgical Press, 2007). And see also Jerome Murphy-O'Connor, *The Holy Land* (Oxford: Oxford University Press, 1980/1992): 13, 31, 36, 110.

or stand in the breach when the walls begin to crumble. Certainly the "living stones" might stand for the purity of religion and against the economic practices that selling things in the Temple ("money changing" in the other gospels) represent, or the corruption of making a holy place, and the only part of the Temple complex to which Gentiles had access, one of commerce. Or we might strive to promote a legal justice that neither the Jewish nor Roman systems of law exhibited at the end of Jesus' life.

The "scattered stones" image of Jerusalem destroyed is bad enough, but it reappears when Jesus predicts the destruction of the Temple itself. To predict the Temple's destruction was to predict the death of the "heart's core" of Second Temple Judaism, the locus of Jewish aspiration, the dwelling place of YHWH. Jesus "was teaching the people in the temple and telling the good news" (Luke 20:1). That "good news" was similar to that of John the Baptist, whose origin Luke treats at length in chapters 1 to 3. The people approved of John, but some of the religious authorities certainly did not. When Jesus in Luke 20:3-4 asks the authority behind John the Baptist's baptism ("from heaven" or "of human origin"), the religious authorities realize either answer gets them in trouble: "[I]f we say, 'Of human origin,' all the people will *stone* us; for they are convinced that John was a prophet" (20:6; italics mine).

Jesus confounds "the chief priest and the scribes" (Luke 20:1), "spies" (20:20), and "some Sadducees" (20:27), and then watches "rich people putting their gifts into the treasury." A "poor widow put in two small copper coins," and Jesus notes she has put in literally "all her life" (21:1-4). The juxtaposition within the next verse is striking. "[S]ome were speaking about the temple, how it was adorned with beautiful *stones* and gifts dedicated to God" (21:5; italics mine). On whose back do those "beautiful stones" rest? Who paid for the beauties of the temple? Those like the widow who were economically most vulnerable? Who is really beautiful? The poor widow or the edifice of the Temple? It is in this context that we hear for the second time "the days will come when not one stone will be left upon another; all will be thrown down" (21:6).

In both these passages the "scattered stones" occur as the result of either unrealized promise or of active corruption and injustice. Jesus weeps because the people God loves (us) have made such a total muddle of God's wonderful plans. Jerusalem was to have been a city of peace, according to Isaiah, a utopian place in which all the nations would gather. But it had not done "the things that make for peace" (19:41). The Temple was to have been a "house of prayer" (19:46; Isa 56:7) but became a "den of robbers" (see Jer 7:11). The physical beauty of Herod's Temple would not, according to Jesus, endure (21:6), and the context of his prediction makes me wonder if its destruction had also to do with injustice in the funding of the "beautiful stones." Both the "widow's mite" and the crushing tax burdens of the Herodian era point in that direction, but we could draw parallels from contemporary events.

The "scattered stones" of the last week of Jesus remind us that what *appears to be* permanent and safe may not be. They ask us to consider on what we are building our lives. *Is* our hope "built on nothing less / than Jesus' blood and righteousness?" *Do* we stand on "Christ, the solid Rock?"[10] Or do we stand on a healthy IRA and stock portfolio? Scattered stones are also a sobering image of what can happen when God's justice is perverted by humans. Luke's is the gospel that opens with Mary's "Magnificat" in which God has mercy on those who fear God, scatters the proud, brings down the powerful, lifts up the lowly, fills the hungry, and helps "his servant Israel, / in remembrance of his mercy," not because Israel is just or obedient but because God is merciful (Luke 1:46-55). The image of "scattered stones" is the other side of the coin of God's mercy; it is God's justice of which the prophets speak and for which the psalmist prays. And what of those "thrown stones" (20:6), which the religious officials fear? Might they be the image of people who take justice into their own hands? Those who seek to obliterate others who hold differing opinions? These old stones are eerily contemporary.

But, of course, at the time Jesus speaks, the predicted total destruction has not yet happened. There is still hope of ecclesial, political, and social reformation. This is the message of the kingdom/reign of God that Jesus came to

10. Phrases from the hymn "The Solid Rock" by Edward Mote (1797–1874).

deliver. There is still the opportunity to "come to [the] living stone," to *become* a living stone "built into a spiritual house" (1 Pet 2:4-5). For me, at least, the ray of light, the "living stone" in these images of crumbling edifice, is the poor widow with her two copper coins, creeping toward a treasure that the powerful, the rich, and those impressed with external appearances cannot even imagine. Of the likes of her God might still be able to build an eternal Zion.

CHAPTER THREE

God's Stony Reversals

(Luke 20:17-18)

What happens when what looks permanent isn't?

The last chapter ended with an image of absolute destruction: not one stone left upon another. I'm afraid the next two chapters also deal with what for some of us may be "scary stones." Please remember this study is of rocks, not rose gardens. We begin this reflection with several questions. I suggest you think about what they imply and your answers to them before you read on. Those reflections will form your backdrop for this chapter's material.

~Question One: What do you do and where do you turn when cracks appear in your foundations, when the foundational aspects of your life are threatened?

~Question Two: What do you do when "things go smash"?

Foundations "rocked" and things "going smash" are what stand behind Luke 20:17-18 in which a defective stone becomes the cornerstone, the basic foundation of the building, which subsequently becomes, more or less, a killer. Quoting Isaiah 8:14-15, Jesus addresses a crowd: "What then does this text mean: 'The stone that the builders rejected / has become the cornerstone?' Everyone who falls on that stone will be broken to pieces; and it will crush anyone on whom it falls."

Context in Luke's Text

Chapter 20 follows from the "triumphal entry"[1] to Jerusalem. Jesus is now regularly teaching in the Temple. The ordinary people (the *laos*) are "spellbound" (19:48); the Greek literally says "they hung on his words," which I think is an extraordinary pun. The chief priests and scribes and leaders, on the other hand, "kept looking for a way to kill him" (Luke 19:47-48). The problem is authority. The people recognize that Jesus has it, but the leaders didn't authorize it. (How dare he preach without a theological degree or a license from the bishop? How dare she minister without the bishop's permission? You get the idea.) Luke makes this explicit at the beginning of chapter 20, which Luke Timothy

---

1. Some recent gospel scholars suggest it wasn't as "triumphal" as our Holy Week liturgies suggest.

Johnson calls "the heart of his story, the spot toward which his narrative has tended, the place of pivot."[2]

Jesus is teaching in the Temple, "telling the good news" (20:1), and the chief priests, scribes, and elders explicitly ask him, "[B]y what authority are you doing these things? Who is it who gave you this authority?" (20:2). They seem most interested in human credentialing. As is characteristic of him, Jesus answers a question with a question that is a total conundrum, one which has two answers, each problematic. "Did the baptism of John come from heaven, or was it of human origin?" (20:4). Luke Timothy Johnson comments that by forcing the religious leaders "to deal with the prophetic ministry of John, he shifts attention from his own credentials to the issue of their openness to God's visitation."[3] What do we do when the Word of God appears in our midst?

The religious leaders are flummoxed, and Jesus is off the hook for the moment. But he turns to the people (the *laon* again) and, in the hearing of the leaders, offers a riff on Isaiah's "Song of the Vineyard" (5:1-7), the parable of the Wicked Tenants (verses 9-18, which also appears in Mark 12:1-12, Matthew 21:33-46, and in a shortened version in the Gospel of Thomas 65).[4] In the Lukan Jesus' version of

2. Luke Timothy Johnson, *The Gospel of Luke*, Sacra Pagina (Collegeville, MN: Liturgical Press, 1991), 307.

3. Johnson, *The Gospel of Luke*, 308.

4. For a helpful reading of the parable, see John Dominic Crossan, "The Parable of the Wicked Husbandmen," *Journal of Biblical Literature* 90 (1971): 451–465.

the parable, after showing extraordinary patience, the vineyard owner deposes the evil tenants who kill his messengers; he "destroys" them and gives the vineyard to others.

As is often the case, Jesus' parable is multivalent; it has several levels of meaning, and our reading depends on whether we think of Jesus' original hearers or Luke's audience or ourselves. For Luke's Greco-Roman, Gentile audience/readers, this is very good news. They must have thought of themselves as those previously excluded from the vineyard. But for Jesus' original hearers there in the Temple, it is very upsetting, *especially* to the religious leaders. So the event closes much as chapter 19 did, with dark foreshadowing: "When the scribes and chief priests realized that he had told this parable against them, they wanted to lay hands on him at that very hour, but they feared the people" (20:19). That Jesus is so often popular with the people may temporarily protect him, but that very fact increases the opposition of the "authorities" both religious and secular.

The "stone verses" are Jesus' summation of the parable. Here is what happens when people act like the tenants in the parable. Jesus directs a "look" that demands attention (verse 17) and says, still in his "questioning-the-hearers mode," "What then does this text mean: 'the stone that the builders rejected / has become the cornerstone'?" Jesus is quoting Psalm 118:22 (117:22, LXX), a text which appears at least five times in the New Testament and probably was widely known as it is from the Hallel, Psalms 113–118, which are chanted at festivals. (Matthew's Jesus quotes the same verse in the same context in 21:42.) Jesus continues, "Everyone who falls on that stone will be broken to pieces; and it will crush anyone on whom it falls" (20:17-18). Falling on the stone is probably an allusion to the "stone of stumbling" in Isaiah 8:14.[5] No wonder the religious authorities are distraught!

The Stone

What we have here is a Trinitarian stone, one stone in three modes: a rejected stone, a cornerstone or keystone, and a crushing stone. Remember that all of the allusions in this text appeared in 1 Peter 2:6-8, a "theme text" for our considerations of the stones of Jesus' last week.

Why would a builder reject a stone? Basically because it was in some fundamental way flawed, chipped, cracked, or the wrong color for the building under construction. Monumental buildings in Jesus' time—like those in Roman Sepphoris, down the road from Nazareth where he grew up, and where, as a *tekton*, a skilled worker, he may have been employed—were built with huge blocks of stone that were cut to fit the construction (like those Temple blocks

5. There the "stone of stumbling" was a trip for "the house of Jacob" and a snare for those who lived in Jerusalem. Those who fell on it would be crushed. See Johnson, 306–307. And, as noted in the first chapter, the literal meaning of the Greek *skandal* or *skandalon* is "something one trips over," something that causes one to fall.

we thought about in the last chapter). A rejected stone was one that, in its original state, was so flawed that it wouldn't be worth chiseling into shape for a building. It couldn't be shaped or sized to fit; it was "a reject." The Greek word *apedokimasan* implies rejection *after* examination. Did Jesus expect his hearers to understand that the builders were the priests, scribes, and elders and that the rejected stone was himself *and* those completely outside the community of Israel, the "misfits," the unclean, the sinners, the Gentiles? If so, the next phrase is exceedingly shocking.

The rejected stone has become the cornerstone or, in some translations, the "keystone" because the Greek literally means "head of the corner." A cornerstone holds things together from the base up and can be used to unite two different walls. A keystone is the central, topmost stone in an arch that holds the others in place. The point for us is that Jesus quotes a text that says the stone judged fundamentally flawed becomes the stone that holds the edifice together. We think of a cornerstone as ceremonial, the stone laid at the formal beginning of the erection of a building. Builders, or those who knew about building at Jesus' time, more probably thought of it as the basic or main stone of the foundation. What characterizes a cornerstone or a keystone is its foundational nature, its function of holding other things together.

Do you suppose Jesus' original hearers understood *he* was the cornerstone the builders were rejecting, that he, himself, was the beginning of a new edifice and what would hold it together? Or did they understand that he was a cornerstone uniting two walls, was holding together the walls of the Law and the Prophets with a *new way*?[6] Or were they, the riffraff and marginalized, being elevated to a new status? Was this a verbal example of the lifting up of the lowly about which Jesus' mother sang in Luke 1:52? Insofar as religious language is multivalent, capable of several levels of meaning, the correct answer to these questions may be that all of them are in some measure true.

Actually, the term *cornerstone* is widely applied to Jesus in the New Testament. If Acts 4:11 is indeed the record of St. Peter's speech to the Jerusalem Council, then Peter applies the "cornerstone" quotation to Jesus. Certainly the writer of 1 Peter 2:6 applies this quotation from Isaiah 28:16 to Jesus:

> "See, I am laying in Zion a stone,
>   a cornerstone chosen and precious;
> and whoever believes in him will not be put to shame."

The writer of Ephesians describes Christian believers as "members of the household of God, built upon the foundation of the apostles and prophets, with Christ Jesus himself as the cornerstone" (Eph 2:19-20). In 1 Corinthians Paul pushes the "Jesus as rock" image right into the Exodus-Sinai account and completely shatters any sense of linear time

---

6. In its reflection on bringing together Gentiles and Jews, the Ephesian letter suggests that Christ "has made both groups into one and has broken down the dividing wall, that is the hostility between us" (Eph 2:14). The wall was almost certainly stone.

when he says "our ancestors"—that is, the Jews—"all ate the same spiritual food, and all drank the same spiritual drink. For they drank from the spiritual rock that followed them, and the rock was Christ" (1 Cor 10:1-4; more on this text in the following excursus).

The flawed, rejected rock becomes the cornerstone. It is the foundation and unifying substance of the building. So far so good. But those who fall on it are broken (literally "shattered"), and those on whom it falls are crushed. *Crushed* is a strong word in English. The Greek word *likmesai* literally means "to winnow chaff from grain, to blow away like chaff, to sweep out of existence." Some scholars think it means "grind to powder."[7] The stone is now, in its third function, a "living stone"; it sifts, which (as noted previously) is a metaphor in the gospels for judgment. (See, for example, Luke 2:17; 22:31.) Luke 20:18 suggests we might think of this stone in the context of judgment texts, stories in which God separates wheat from chaff or sheep from goats. It echoes the harsh reality at the end of the parable Jesus has just told. The vineyard owner destroys the wicked tenants. The irony is that what the builders rejected ends up with the authority to judge the builders themselves.

The stark images of 20:16 and 20:18 are images of God's justice, a divine characteristic of which Luke is particularly fond. His gospel begins with it in Mary's Magnificat

7. Fritz Rienecker and Cleon Rogers, *Linguistic Key to the Greek New Testament* (Grand Rapids, MI: Regency/Zondervan Publishing, 1976/1980), 201.

in chapter 1:47-55. The Mighty One looks with favor on the lowly, does great things for them, lifts up the lowly, brings down the powerful, sends away the rich.

These particular metaphorical stones in the last week of Jesus remind us that God is a God of justice, and divine justice involves some shocking reversals. In light of the parable of the Wicked Tenants, it suggests that those to whom the vineyard were entrusted forgot that it didn't belong to them, mistreated and killed the owner's messengers, and, in the end, are very seriously demoted by the owner. In the context in which the story is told, it's a case in point of the mighty being brought down from their thrones, and the mighty, the religio-political leadership represented by the chief priests and scribes, absolutely "get" the message. They realize that Jesus "had told this parable against them" (Luke 20:19). This stone is a sobering reminder that all of us will be called to account for what has been entrusted to us. The Lukan Jesus has already said, "From everyone to whom much has been given, much will be required; and from the one to whom much has been entrusted, even more will be demanded" (12:48).

This particular stone is in the business of building up, of judging, and of crushing. I once heard a genius described as someone who can hold two conflicting ideas in mind without having to reconcile them.[8] By that definition, the teller of this parable with its stony conclusion is a genius.

8. This line is F. Scott Fitzgerald's: "The test of a first-rate intelligence is the ability to hold two opposed ideas in the mind at the same time, and still retain the ability to function." From a 1936 essay titled "The Crack-Up":

Application

So where does all this leave us? What practical conclusions can we draw or spiritual insights can we glean? Let me suggest four, two theological and two practical or spiritual.

Theological

1. Jesus is the outsider, the broken stone who is the foundation or keystone of something new that he will hold together. The Temple authorities recognize that this upstart teacher or rabbi from Nazareth in Galilee, a town from which nothing good was expected (John 1:46) and a mixed-racial area not known for religious purity, is passing judgment on the religious establishment, and they behave exactly as people who have public power usually do. When it is threatened, their response is not to question themselves but to get rid of the threat. This is the same response the crowd has to them in 20:26. The refusal to engage in self-examination can lead to suffering for others, and violence begets violence.

Whether or not Jesus viewed himself as the beginning of a new theological understanding, much less of a new religious tradition, is open to debate. But certainly Luke, and certainly Paul and the early church understood Jesus in this way. And if they listened carefully, Luke's Greco-Roman audience would have heard in this story another instance

---

https://www.pbs.org/wnet/americanmasters/f-scott-fitzgerald-essay-the-crack-up/1028/.

of their inclusion. The rejected stones were being included in the building.

2. The "triune stone" in this text precludes any hint of a "happy clappy" Christianity or a "buddy-buddy" relationship with God. The vineyard owner has entrusted the tenants with a wonderful gift, and they have abused not only it but the owner's messengers and, therefore, the owner because in their culture the messenger *was* (represented) the owner. (A basic insight in St. John's theology and gospel is that one who brings the master's message represents the master.) The owner is, indeed, kind and generous, but he is also just. The image of God to which the parable alludes does not exclude judgment.

This puts me in mind of two things. First, God's judgment (here the breaking and crushing) is a manifestation of justice. We do not live in a "tit for tat" moral universe in which the good always prosper and the evil always lose out. Nor do we live in a universe in which God is blind to innocent suffering and evil action. In the light of current events (in any age), we can take comfort in the fact that the last chapter of human history hasn't been written but that when it is, a just God will write it.

Second, it pains me to think about it, but in this story *I* might be the religious authorities. When the last chapter of human history is written, *I* might be implicated in the evil to which I have been blind or from which I have averted my eyes. When it comes to judgment, I may be the one who is judged to be the goat and not the sheep. The invitation to me is constantly to examine my own life and actions and the thoughts of the heart from which they proceed. And this sobering point provides the transition to the two practical/ spiritual suggestions offered by this particular stone.

Spiritual

3. The stone is flawed. It starts out being rejected by the builders. It doesn't start out obviously attractive, useable, and perfect. For me this is *really* good news. When God looks at the impermanent and impermeable lump of messy and imperfect stuff that I am, God does, indeed, see the fundamental flaw, the invisible cracks in the fabric, the unsuitable color, the impossible size. But unlike the builders in the text, God does not reject. God makes a most remarkable choice in using me as a stone in the edifice of "living stones" of which Christ's church is built. And God can do the same with you.

You don't have to be a perfect stone to be useful in God's building project. You just have to be willing to be used. "For we are," the Ephesian letter asserts, "what [God] has made us" (2:10a), flaws and all. I have come to think that it is precisely our *imperfections* that make us most readily available to the Master Builder. When I am full of my gifts and strengths, it is easy to think I am the source of what I offer, that I *own* the vineyard and can dispose of its produce myself. But when I am in a mess, or *am* a mess, well aware of my flaws and imperfections and downright cussedness, in some mysterious way I am more available to God, more malleable, more useful. There is a profound truth in an old hymn by Adelaide Pollard that echoes an image in Hebrew Scripture:

> Have thine own way, Lord! Have thine own way!
> Thou are the potter; I am the clay.
> Mold me and make me after thy will
> While I am waiting, yielded and still.[9]

The potter begins with what is, in essence, a lump of wet dirt and makes of it something useful and/or beautiful. God can use the profoundly imperfect, the wounded, and the weary. But we must yield to God's shaping hand. A profound surrender, one that can be very costly, is required. For most of us, surrender is not easy. We only run up our white flag after a long siege.

4. Finally, the stone we have been considering is foundational. It's the cornerstone or the keystone, that which holds the building together either from the bottom or from the top. Practically speaking, every life needs a cornerstone or a keystone, a particular point of stability from which that life can be built.

In the two questions with which this chapter began, I assumed this basic point. If you could begin to think about so frightening a thing as the shaking of your foundations, it means that you have some to begin with. One of life's great

9. Adelaide Addison Pollard, "Have Thine Own Way, Lord" (1862–1934).

challenges is periodically to reexamine what it is built upon. To use the familiar Pauline mixed metaphor of "rooted and grounded," we might ask ourselves how and where we are really rooted. What is our foundation and provides our stability? What nurtures us?[10]

This chapter's stone presents us with a shocking reversal: that which seemed damaged is, in fact, the foundational stone. The great religious edifice upon which so many lives were built, and for which the priests and scribes and elders are but one image, is proving to be rather precarious. Jesus invites us to consider our foundations and, *if* they are wobbly, to be open to the possibility that we've built on sand rather than rock. And if *that* is the case, then we get busy with rebuilding, knowing that God's stony reversals promise that no bad decision is irreversible and no stone too flawed to be reclaimed for the reign of God, the kingdom Christ is building.

10. One can see this process bravely undertaken by reading the American Episcopal priest and professor Barbara Brown Taylor's work in chronological order. Read the sermons, then *Leaving Church: A Memoir of Faith* (New York: HarperOne, 2006), *An Altar in the World: A Geography of Faith* (New York: HarperOne, 2009), and *Learning to Walk in the Dark* (New York: HarperOne, 2014).

A Hidden Stone?

(Luke 22:14-23)

At this point, Gentle Reader, you will have realized that, in the interpretation of Holy Scripture, this writer has a metaphorical or poetic cast of mind. This will be especially evident in the following brief excursus, which posits a "hidden stone" in the last week of Jesus' life and an invisible stone in the next chapter. I hope neither is eisegesis, "reading into" the text things that aren't there, but a gentle "breaking open" of Scripture that reveals the beauty of its multivalency. At any rate, the following is how the possibility of a hidden stone revealed itself to me.

I was reading Evelyn Underhill's classic book *Worship* (in an attempt to negotiate the complexities of pandemic liturgy). In chapter 11, "The Beginnings of Christian Worship," I encountered the following two luminous phrases: "[M]ystery, hiddenness, was from the beginning inherent in Christian worship" and "Christian ritual pattern . . . tended

51

to clothe itself in symbolic garments, and express its living secret by symbolic acts."[1] These statements prefaced Underhill's discussion of the primitive Eucharist and its ability to hold together both its sacrificial aspects from Judaism and the concept of Divine Logos from Hellenistic thought, which she notes "was primarily the religious genius of St. Paul."[2] The "Jewish convert," she suggested, "found in the Eucharist a spiritual manna, and there drank from the spiritual Rock."[3] The reference is to 1 Corinthians 10:4: "[T]hey drank from the spiritual rock . . . and the rock was Christ." The "spiritual rock" is the "invisible stone" of the Last Week.

All three synoptic gospels include passages that describe the institution of the Lord's Supper, Jesus' last meal with his followers that we now celebrate as the Eucharist. Luke's account of it diverges in several ways from Mark and Matthew (another discussion for another time) but includes the event in 22:14-23 that Jesus explicitly calls a "Passover" (22:15). In the longer account of this meal (22:7-38), Jesus makes a number of references to Jewish practice and Scripture.[4] After the resurrection, how could the early Christians have

1. Evelyn Underhill, *Worship* (New York: Harper & Row Torchbook, 1936/1957), 238.

2. Underhill, *Worship*, 239.

3. Underhill, *Worship*, 239.

4. In her book *The Altar Fire: Reflections on the Sacrament of the Eucharist* (London: SCM Press, 1954), Olive Wyon draws parallels with many Hebrew scriptures and Jewish rites and sacrificial practices.

missed the connection between the Lord's Supper and the manna in the wilderness? Early Christians in the Johannine community or with access to John's gospel might well recall that Jesus says of himself, "I am the living bread that came down from heaven" (6:51). He goes on to make explicit comparison between himself and "the bread that came down from heaven . . . which your ancestors ate" (6:58).

Relevant to this discussion is the fact that someone called Luke was closely associated with the travels and ministry of St. Paul. A Luke is mentioned in Colossians 4:14, 2 Timothy 4:11, and Philemon 24. Barbara Reid notes that "[d]istinct from the rest of Acts are four passages (16:10-17; 20:5-15; 21:1-18; 27:12–28:16) in which the author speaks in the first-person plural. These 'we sections' came either from a travel diary of the author . . . or from another of Paul's associates . . . or possibly they were composed by Luke."[5] The author of the book of Acts was the evangelist Luke. The first of these "we" passages in Acts 16 describe Paul's second missionary journey, which included the city of Corinth. Paul's first letter to the church in Corinth, which predates John's gospel by a generation, clearly associated manna, water from the rock, and Jesus.

At the outset of 1 Corinthians 10, Paul introduces the practices of baptism and the Lord's Supper by means of

---

5. Barbara E. Reid, "Introduction to The Acts of the Apostles," in *The New Interpreter's Study Bible*, ed. Walter Harrelson (Nashville: Abingdon Press, 2003), 1954.

clear comparisons to the Exodus experience of Israel:
"[A]ll passed through the sea . . . and all ate the same
spiritual food, and all drank the same spiritual drink. For
they drank from the spiritual *rock* that followed them, and
the *rock* was Christ" (1 Cor 10:1, 3-4; italics mine). Jerome
Murphy-O'Connor notes that "instead of using the terms
'manna' and 'water' he speaks of 'spiritual food' and 'spiritual drink.'" He continues, "There is no question of logical
necessity. Paul relies on an instinctive association of ideas in
the minds of those familiar with components of the Eucharist (11:26; *Didache* 10:3)."[6] In the only passage in the New
Testament in which the two sacraments appear together, the
Red Sea prefigured baptism, and manna and "water from
the rock" prefigured Eucharist.[7] In both, divine assistance
and sustenance is provided for a journey.

In his commentary on the passage, J. Paul Sampley ex-
plains that St. Paul's comparison works by mean of typology.
St. Paul takes a past event (here the Exodus) and "*a selective
retelling* of the old story [becomes] a vehicle for guidance
in the present." Typology may "make some explicit link
to . . . readers, but [it] invites readers to make their own
connections as well." Sampley thinks that Paul is "retrofit-
ting baptism and the Lord's supper motifs onto the old

6. Jerome Murphy-O'Connor, *1 Corinthians*, New Testament Message
series (Collegeville, MN: Liturgical Press, 1979/1991), 94.

7. Archibald Robertson and Alfred Plummer, *A Critical and Exegetical
Commentary on the First Epistle of Paul to the Corinthians*, International
Critical Commentary (New York: Charles Scribner's Sons, 1911), 202.

story. . . . Even the rock from which they drank (Exodus
17:6; Numbers 20:11) is identified as Christ (10:4b)."[8] A bit
more about Christ as the rock is in order.

First, in several epistles, Paul (or one of his disciples)
speaks explicitly of a preexistent Christ, suggesting that
"Christ" existed before the incarnation. (See, for example,
Philippians 2:6-7 or Colossians 1:15-16.[9]) Robertson and
Plumber suggest 1 Corinthians 10:4 is "unquestionable evi-
dence of the Apostle's belief in the pre-existence of Christ."[10]
Second, and relatedly, in 1 Corinthians 10:4, "the spiritual
rock . . . followed them." (A very good trick indeed for a
rock!) This is an allusion to a Jewish legend that the water-
giving rock followed the Israelites in the desert.[11] Third,
F. F. Bruce and others point out "the use of the title 'The
Rock' for Yahweh" in Hebrew Scripture.[12] And for Philo,

8. J. Paul Sampley, "The First Letter to the Corinthians," in *The New
Interpreter's Bible Commentary*, ed. Leander E. Keck (Nashville: Abingdon, 2002), X:913–914.

9. Other examples are found in 2 Corinthians 8:9, Galatians 4:4, and
Romans 8:3. And compare John 1:1-3 for the same idea, which must have
had traction in the churches in Greece and Asia Minor.

10. Robertson and Plummer, *A Critical and Exegetical Commentary*,
201.

11. Pseudo-Philo, *Biblical Antiquities* x.7; Tosefta *Sukkah* iii. 11ff.
And see discussion in Robertson and Plummer, *A Critical and Exe-
getical Commentary*, 201–202, and in F. F. Bruce, *I & II Corinthians*, New
Century Bible Commentary (Grand Rapids, MI: Eerdmans, 1971), 91.

12. Deut 32:4, 15, 18, 30, 31; Ps 18:2, 31; 19:14; 28:1 (and several other
references); Isa 26:4.

"'the flinty rock is the wisdom of God'. . . the manna is the word of God."[13]

A number of New Testament scholars have pointed out that some of the evangelists depict Jesus as Wisdom as Wisdom is depicted in Hebrew Scripture. As a Pauline example, Sampley writes, "Philo. . . contemporary with Paul, identified the rock as Wisdom, who, thus personified, never abandoned God's people. As the Lord's supper's food and drink are retrofitted back onto the old story so is Christ."[14] Christ as Rock (both a metaphor for God and symbol of Wisdom) from whom comes living water is certainly an example of Evelyn Underhill's observation that early Christian thinking "tended to clothe itself in symbolic garments."[15]

I'm not suggesting that in 22:19-20 Luke *expected* the reader to make the connection between the elements of the Eucharist and the manna provided for Israel in the wilderness. There is nothing in Luke's text, per se, that would support such an assertion. But it is the case that early Christians *had* made that connection. Certainly Paul, with whom Luke is traditionally associated, made the connection explicitly in 1 Corinthians 10, which was written some thirty years before Luke's gospel, in plenty of time for the letter's ideas

13. Philo *Leg. Alleg.* Ii.86, iii. 169ff. Quoted in Bruce, *I & II Corinthians*, 91. And see Robertson and Plummer, *A Critical and Exegetical Commentary*, 201–202.

14. Sampley, "The First Letter to the Corinthians," 915.

15. Underhill, *Worship*, 238.

and instructions to circulate. I simply suggest that there is no reason why a Jewish Christian or a former God-fearer or a Gentile who had read or been instructed in Hebrew Scripture *couldn't* have made the connections on which 1 Corinthians 10:1-4 depend.

You may or may not be inclined to include this particular "stone" at the Last Supper in Jesus' last week. If you do so, you are including, in what must have been a traumatic week for Jesus and his first followers, a stony reminder that, in life's deserts, in the difficult stages of life's journey, God provided and continues to provide heavenly sustenance, what the Johannine Jesus describes as "the bread that comes down from heaven" (John 6:41, 50) and what St. Paul called spiritual drink from the rock that is Christ (1 Cor 10:1-4).[16] It's another way that, in the words of the African American spiritual, "God is a rock in a weary land." Everywhere, in every weary land, God provides life's necessary water.

16. The book of Revelation also associates Christ with life-giving water. See, for example, 7:17; 21:6; 22:1. And see John 4 on "living water."

CHAPTER FOUR

A Stone's Throw Away

(Luke 22:41)

How close are we willing to get to suffering?

"[Jesus] withdrew from them about a stone's throw, knelt down, and prayed." (Luke 22:41)

We have walked the stony road of Jesus' last week, visited the night of the institution of the Lord's Supper (which the excursus suggested had a "stone" component), and now come to the Garden of Gethsemane and the betrayal of Jesus. This is one of the rockiest parts of the journey, and the biggest stone connected with it in our minds may be one that doesn't exist.

The church in which I grew up in Beckley, West Virginia, had lovely stained-glass windows. One wall of the sanctuary had huge depictions of things like Jesus with the woman at the well. But my favorite window was up in the shadows of the balcony against the back wall. It was a scene you may recognize. Jesus is on his knees, his body leaning against a great, dark rock, his elbows propped on it with his hands clasped in prayer (just like they taught us in Sunday School). The ground around him is grey. The sky is sort of navy blue. The only light in the window is Jesus' face and white robe. Even a child knew that his prayer was about something very serious indeed.

I expect I'm not the only one who has that image, or one very like it, in mind when the Garden of Gethsemane is mentioned. It is ubiquitous in Western art and, by the way, is also found in the iconographers of the East, who frame the scene with craggy rocks, which are one way the iconographer says "theophany." But when I carefully read the synoptic gospels (St. John omits the Garden of Gethsemane event), I find that particular rock isn't explicitly mentioned. Mark's gospel says Jesus threw himself on the ground (14:35). Matthew echoes Mark exactly (26:39), and Luke alludes to it when he describes Jesus as getting "up from prayer" (22:45). Somehow, in the human minds of artists and believers, the idea has taken root that, *in extremis*, even Jesus had to lean on something. I'll return to that later.

In fact, the "stone" of Gethsemane occurs only in Luke (who has several divergences from the other synoptics). It describes distance, not substance—how far away from Jesus the accompanying disciples are. Luke has just described the Last Supper, which, for his Greco-Roman audience, he has cast as a symposium with Jesus offering final teachings and closing with one that apparently excludes violent responses on the part of his followers. Then Jesus goes out "as was his custom, to the Mount of Olives" (22:39). Luke's is the gospel that most frequently depicts Jesus as withdrawing for prayer, so the action would not particularly have alarmed his followers, whom he also charges to pray (22:40).

Unlike Mark and Matthew, Luke doesn't single out the "inner circle" of Peter, James, and John, but has the wider group of "disciples," not just the Twelve, accompany him. So we are to understand his charge in 22:40 as applying to all his followers (including the women and us): "Pray that you may not come into the time of trial." The word for "trial" is *peirasmon*, the same word we pray in the Lord's Prayer when we say "lead us not into temptation," that is, into the final testing. What is in view here is not martinis, rich desserts, and sexual misconduct, but "the big one," the end times' challenge described in Matthew 24–25, Mark 13, and Luke's own previous chapter. *Now* we encounter the stone, and it is apparently a rather small one, not the boulder of my stained-glass window: "Then [Jesus] withdrew from them about a stone's throw, knelt down, and prayed" (22:41).

Some ancient manuscripts of Luke's gospel (which has a complex textual history) describe that prayer as accompanied by great physical suffering, sweating blood. But our question is: How far can you throw a stone? I suppose it depends upon who you are and how big the stone is. The masculine and muscular might be able to throw it some distance,

but not out of sight (unless he is Superman). Softball pitch-
ers might not achieve a great distance with an underhand
throw. I think Luke's point in saying "about a stone's throw"
is to suggest "not very far." Those who accompanied Jesus
could, if not overhear the prayer, at least see its intensity and
its suffering, rather like I did as a child sneaking up to the
balcony to look at that stained-glass window.

I have been to the Garden of Gethsemane several times
(once on a Maundy Thursday night) and can report it *is* a
rocky place where there *are* big rocks against which Jesus
might have leaned. The Church of All Nations there is
built around one. Luke's depiction of Jesus in the Garden
of Gethsemane raises another question, one of particular
relevance to us who lived through the COVID-19 pandemic. How close are we willing to get to suffering? How
much distance do we put between ourselves and suffering?
What's the "stone's throw" for us when it comes to the suffering in the world around us?

Honestly, I quite understand the disciples' need to sleep.
It *had* been an exhausting week for them. They *were* tired.
And they were also human as we are and probably were
uneasy about being in the presence of great suffering or,
truth be told, of suffering themselves (as their imminent
departure from the scene indicates). Unless we are psychologically disordered, we don't like to suffer ourselves, and
most of us don't like to be in the presence of those who are
suffering. We actively try to avoid both. And I wonder if
this is entirely spiritually healthy for us.

Before I continue, let me assure you that I am not about to espouse masochism. I am not in favor of unnecessary suffering or self-inflicted suffering. Life provides plenty of opportunities to suffer. We need not manufacture them. And in any case, all the *required* suffering in the universe has already been done by Jesus on the cross. I'm in favor of hospices ensuring that the dying are comfortable. I'm grateful for psychotropic drugs that alleviate the suffering of mental illness. Please don't misunderstand. What I am about to say has to do with a rather different aspect or level of experience. It is this: I'm not sure that the avoidance of all suffering is good for the hearts of Christian disciples. Total avoidance of suffering might turn hearts of flesh back into hearts of stone.

If you don't believe that we actively seek to avoid suffering, I invite you to stop by any pharmacy and wander down the pain remedies aisle and notice how many medications there are. I invite you to think about how often in the course of a week you reach for a pain medication or a glass of wine or some other pain-masking substance. I wonder what it does to one over a lifetime to mask all our physical and psychological pain. I'm not a physician, but my own body has taught me that pain can be a great blessing in that, first, it alerts me to the fact that something is amiss, and, if I block it out, I might be ignoring an important signal. Second, if I always stop pain the moment it begins (even before I know if it is going to be serious or merely niggling), I lose an opportunity to learn something about compassion for those who live with chronic pain: physical or psychological or spiritual. Consistently masking my own pain might prevent me from learning compassion for someone else's. (Remember, I'm not suggesting masochism.)

Always inuring ourselves to another's pain is worrisome. How close are we willing to get to suffering? "Not very close" is the answer our culture gives. If you've read much about World War I, you know that the war didn't end with the armistice or when the soldiers went home. No war ever does, but that one taught us about "shell shock," which is related to what we now call post-traumatic stress disorder. One case in point: some men were so terribly wounded and scarred by the war and its hideous new weapons that in the United Kingdom institutions were developed so that the war-warped and scarred could live together and not be seen and stared at in public. Families kept their war-deformed at home to protect them from the horrified stares of onlookers.

We can do something like this, can't we? Sometimes we institutionalize those who suffer so that we don't have to see them. That may be a blessed thing. I am thinking in particular of Cregg House, in Sligo, Ireland, a ministry founded by the Daughters of Wisdom, a Roman Catholic religious order. That house was built to care lovingly for children too physically and psychologically damaged and challenged to be at home or in mainstream schools. I have seldom seen such love: the sisters for the children and the children for the sisters. So again, don't misunderstand what I am saying here.

But hiding suffering can be as much for our comfort as for that of the sufferers, can't it? We don't want to be confronted by the diminishment and difficulties of aging, so we build "homes" with disingenuous names like "Happy Valley" and "Golden Days." If we happen to see on the street someone who is badly crippled or facially scarred, some of us cross over to the other side so that we don't have to meet the person's eyes. Most of us avoid the psychologically damaged, especially those who are off their meds. I have a hard time looking at those who beg, especially at a one-legged chap at an intersection I often traverse, but I am training myself to do so. (By the way, his cardboard sign says he is offering "free tickets to heaven," and I could do with one of those.)

Be honest. Take a moment to think about the ways you avoid suffering. Maybe you take too many aspirin. Maybe you use that favorite psychological pain killer, alcohol—or ice cream or chocolates—to excess. Maybe you don't call that recent widow because she reminds you at some unspeakable level that she might be *you*. Maybe you avoid the person with long-term cancer because you don't know what to say. He makes you uncomfortable, never mind the discomforts of *his* long-term treatments. Maybe it's easier not to think about Christians being martyred in Iraq or Libya, easier not to know about Ebola in Africa or Syrian refugees in unspeakable camps, the slaughter of innocents in Gaza, or unaccompanied children in cages, easier not to think about domestic violence or abused children closer to home. Maybe it's better to turn off the television news and watch a cheering, happily-ever-after Hallmark movie than to confront our own psychological or spiritual suffering or internal emptiness.

How close are we willing to get to suffering? How close was Jesus willing to get to suffering? If I read the gospels correctly, the answer is "very, very close." He looks and speaks and touches those whom others could and did avoid. One of his most beloved parables, that of the Good Samaritan, found only in Luke (10:29-37), is about just this. Jesus practiced compassion. The word for "compassion" in Greek is an interesting one: *splagnizomai.* The root word *splagna* means, literally, "guts" or probably more specifically "an empty space inside," such as a "womb." Jesus has a "gut feeling," a "womb feeling," the feeling of a mother for her children when he sees suffering. Jesus not only recognized suffering, but he *practiced* compassion; he entered into it. Discipleship invites us to do the same thing: to practice looking at and reaching out to what we might otherwise turn away from and avoid. We might start by seeing the face of Christ in the suffering closest to home.[1] Practicing compassion is practicing Christ-likeness, and as the old saw goes, "Practice makes perfect."

But what if we, you or I, *are* the sufferer? What if we're the one others turn from because our mental quirks or physical limitations or chronic illness frighten them? When

1. The visionary experiences of the twentieth-century Roman Catholic spiritual writer and artist Caryll Houselander were of the face of Christ in the faces of others.

someone turns away from me, it diminishes my sense of self, my self-respect, my sense of value. Many of us live in cultures where only those who can produce are valued, which is why our society's public policy largely ignores the welfare of children and the elderly. They aren't economically productive. If my suffering precludes my "usefulness," I am valueless; so goes the tacit understanding.

But there are two pieces of good news here. First, *Jesus never* turns away from those who suffer. As Rabbi Abraham J. Heschel so eloquently asserts in discussing "divine pathos" in his book *The Prophets*, God is not immutable or unmoved by human suffering.[2] God suffers with the suffering, as Elie Weisel so very dramatically taught us in his writing on the Holocaust. When we experience some kinds of suffering, our best strategy may not be to reach for the aspirin or spiral into self-loathing or change the channel on the TV, but to open ourselves totally to the God who suffered for and with us. Inviting God into our suffering can radically transform it.

Second, ours is a crucified God. As Paul said, "[W]e proclaim Christ crucified, a stumbling block to Jews and foolishness to Gentiles, but to those who are the called, both Jews and Greeks, Christ the power of God and the wisdom of God" (1 Cor 1:23-24). This implies that the power and wisdom of God was *in* Christ's crucifixion. The cross of Jesus Christ proclaims that no suffering is meaningless or

2. Abraham J. Heschel, *The Prophets: An Introduction* (New York: Harper Torchbooks, 1955).

potentially unredeemable. Sr. Maria Boulding reminds us that Paul "had come to preach a crucified Christ, and the message had to be embodied in the messenger if the hearers were to recognize the truth of Christ's cross and resurrection, and know Easter life in themselves." Thus, "Paul's suffering was necessary; it was the condition that made the weakness and death of Jesus present."[3]

Boulding calls this "the folly of God's paschal methods."[4] It suggests to me that *suffering itself* is a gift we have to bring, perhaps the most powerful one. Perhaps, to use an old Roman Catholic phrase which, sadly, is often mocked, suffering *is* what we have to "offer up." In this context, it is well worth pondering Paul's mysterious words to the church at Colossae: "I am now rejoicing in my sufferings *for your sake*, and in my flesh I am completing what is lacking in Christ's affliction *for the sake of his body . . . the church*" (Col 1:24; italics mine).

Some of us are old enough to remember the original Christmas Eve broadcast in the United States in 1951 of Giancarlo Menotti's opera *Amahl and the Night Visitors*. We remember how the kings visited the hovel of a poor widow and her crippled son, how she was tempted to steal a little of the riches meant for the Child they sought in order to help

3. Maria Boulding, OSB, *Gateway to Resurrection* (London: Burns & Oates, 2010), 22. And recall that in the Greco-Roman world in which Jesus resided, a proof of the truth of a teacher's message was that the teacher embodied or lived it out.

4. Boulding, *Gateway to Resurrection*, 23.

her own son. Do you remember when the plot turned? It was when little, crippled Amahl asked to go with the kings *so he could give his crutch to the Christ child*. What Amahl had to give was his suffering, his crutch. The child who led them all couldn't even walk unaided.

I am convinced that sometimes precisely what God needs is what Amahl offered—not my strengths or goodness or gifts or riches, but my suffering. Offering God my suffering and brokenness is the outward and visible sign of my surrender to God. This is what God may want to hear me say: "I can't cope with this on my own. Help me. Lord, I'm a total mess, but I'm *your* mess."[5] We might remember this when we hear the Lenten biblical readings about God not being interested in our burnt offerings and the flocks of our fields, the ancient equivalent of riches. God wants more of us than our "stuff," and if our suffering is what we have to offer, that is acceptable. One recalls the power of Caryll Houselander's assertion in *The Reed of God* (written in the midst of the suffering of World War II) that what God wanted from Mary of Nazareth was Mary. "She had nothing to give Him but herself. / He asked for nothing else."[6]

I hope I have made a convincing case that in our society the suffering are devalued and that this affects the sufferers' own sense of self-worth. "I'm too sick to work, so I'm no

5. Perhaps in this context, some of us remember the Billy Graham altar call hymn, "Just as I Am," by Charlotte Elliott (1789–1971).

6. Caryll Houselander, *The Reed of God* (Allen, TX: Christian Classics, 1976), 28.

good, without value." "I'm so badly scarred that I must be useless." Can anyone who stands before the cross of Jesus Christ hold such evil (yes, evil) views? Writing about the sick, M. Marie des Douleurs (foundress of the Congregation of the Benedictines of Jesus Crucified) said, "The mission of the sick person is to give witness to the cross." She points out that many people avoid suffering. She calls *them* "the living dead." She writes, "The sick person wakes people up."[7] We were not created to be the "walking dead."

Suffering can wake us up. Our own suffering asks us to attend to ourselves both physically and spiritually, to discern what is wrong and to do what we can to improve it, precisely because Jesus came to give us life and give it in abundance (see John 10:10). Relatedly, by the Sheep Gate in Jerusalem Jesus encountered a man who had been ill for thirty-eight years and asked him, "Do you want to be made well?" (John 5:6). Unfortunately, some who are sick resist healing because they experience some "benefit" or "payoff" in illness. It might be easier to sit by the pool than to have to take up my mat and stand on my own two feet.

Being open to the suffering of others can give us the great gifts of remembering the cross and of practicing compassion. To turn away from suffering is to develop the most dangerous of spiritual problems: a calloused heart. All of the world's suffering says to the Christian, "Look at me. I

---

7. Quoted in *Magnificat* 16, no. 12 (February 2015): 158.

am the face of your Lord." Maybe as a child I used to slip up to that small, arc-shaped, stained-glass window of Jesus in the garden precisely to see his face, the face I saw in my classmates who didn't have lunch or coats in the winter and whose faces I remember when I have the privilege of bagging groceries at the food pantry where I volunteer.

For those of you who will dare to draw near to suffering, I have another question: What will be the rock that you lean on? Because if you enter into your own suffering and the suffering of others, you are going to need support. That big rock that Jesus leans on in artists' renderings of Gethsemane may not be in the gospel accounts, but I think it is spiritually important as we enter suffering, especially, perhaps, in Holy Week when we are liturgically invited to enter Jesus' suffering. That rock is an image of support or stability. It occurs dozens of times in the Psalms. Perhaps it's the physical manifestation of the popular song by Bill Withers "Lean on Me." Perhaps the rock that Jesus leaned on in Gethsemane was prayer itself and the One to whom it was addressed. Prayer was the rock that supported and strengthened and gave courage to Jesus in the suffering he (quite healthily) asked to be spared, knowing by this time that it wouldn't play out that way. Prayer was the rock that supported and strengthened Jesus in his physical and psychological suffering and in the suffering he must have known his choices would cause his Mother, his friends, and his disciples.

"How close are you willing to get to suffering?" is a very potent question for us Christians who always live in the shadow of Good Friday or of the Cross, which radically changes the meaning of suffering and the value of sufferers. "What is the rock that you lean on?" may be the question that sustains us as we embrace both the suffering that may be our greatest gift to offer and the sufferers who will keep the chambers of our hearts open.

The haunting words from King Melchior's aria near the end of *Amahl and the Night Visitors* provide both comfort and challenge to us who watch and pray "a stone's throw away."

> The Child we seek doesn't need our gold.
> On love, on love alone
> He will build his Kingdom.
> His pierced hand will hold no scepter.
> His haloed head will wear no crown.
> His might will not be built on your toil.
> Swifter than lightening
> He will soon walk among us.
> He will bring us new life
> and receive our death,
> and the keys to His city
> belong to the poor.
> Let us leave, my friends.[8]

8. Giancarlo Menotti, *Amahl and the Night Visitors*, liner notes from the original cast recording (RCA/BMG Music, 1952), 21–22.

CHAPTER FIVE

The Crucial Dual-Purpose Stone

(Luke 23:52; 24:2; 1 Peter 2:9-10)

Stones and their removal. Tombs and their emptying.

The final two stones on the "road we trod" with Jesus in his last week may be the most important of all. They are the stones that summarize the earliest Christian *kerygma*, the proclamation of its astonishing and empowering message: Jesus died, was buried, was raised, and appeared. St. Paul proclaims this "as of first importance": "Christ died for our sins in accordance with the scriptures, and . . . he was buried, and . . . he was raised on the third day in accordance with the scriptures, and . . . he appeared" (1 Cor 15:3-5). The same four points occur in St. Peter's first sermon on Pentecost as Luke presents it in Acts 2, as well as in other places in the New Testament. These four assertions became central in the

Nicene Creed, which is included in many of Christendom's liturgies: Jesus Christ "suffered death and was buried. On the third day he rose again in accordance with the Scriptures."

"No faith, in the New Testament," Rowan Williams writes, "seems to be definable or identifiable independently of the resurrection."[1] Both Sts. Peter and Paul declare the centrality of what they believed to be the fact of Jesus' resurrection. "This Jesus God raised up, and of that all of us are witnesses," Peter declared at Pentecost (Acts 2:32). In 1 Corinthians 15, Paul's great "resurrection chapter," the apostle puts it very bluntly: "[I]f Christ has not been raised, then our proclamation has been in vain and your faith has been in vain" (15:14). "If Christ has not been raised, your faith is futile" (15:17).

Died. Buried. Raised. Appeared. These four verbs summarize Christian faith and are closely connected, their actions profoundly intertwined. Jesus died. That he was *really* dead is indicated by the fact that he was buried in a tomb sealed with a stone. Matthew's gospel reports Pilate's charge to the soldiers about Jesus' tomb: "[M]ake it as secure as you can." The guard "made the tomb secure by sealing the stone" (Matt 27:65-66). Nevertheless, Jesus was raised. That he returned from the dead was suggested by the fact that the stone that closed the tomb *moved*. The women who went to the tomb the first day of the week found "that the stone, which was very large, had already been rolled back"

---

1. Rowan Williams, *God with Us* (London: SPCK, 2017), 73.

(Mark 16:4; Luke 24:2 and John 20:1 echo Mark). Matthew reports "an angel of the Lord . . . came and rolled back the stone" (Matt 28:2). For the evangelists, that Jesus subsequently appeared to a number of people who had known him (and who were known to some recipients of St. Paul's letters and the gospels), prove Jesus' resurrection. (See, for example, Luke 24, John 20–21, and Acts 1.) Central to the earliest Christian proclamation are buried and raised, both of which involved the same big stone.

The stone that closed Jesus' tomb and proved he was buried was the same stone that was found rolled away and signaled his resurrection. It was a dual-purpose stone. It sealed a death and signaled a resurrection. Mysteriously it offers an image of cosmic ambiguity, of spiritual paradox. Before we briefly explore that, we need to consider the two functions of that astonishing, single stone.

The Stone of Death

"This man went to Pilate and asked for the body of Jesus. Then he took it down, wrapped it in a linen cloth, and laid it in a rock-hewn tomb" (Luke 23:52, 53).

The gospels uniformly report that the burial of Jesus was facilitated by Joseph of Arimathea who provided the tomb. Each gospel treats that burial slightly differently,[2]

2. See Matt 27:57-66; Mark 15:42-47; Luke 23:50-56; John 19:38-42.

but all three synoptic gospels mention a tomb hewn from rock (see Matt 27:60, Luke 23:53, and Mark 15:46). Mark notes that Joseph of Arimathea "rolled a stone against the door of the tomb" (15:46), a "stone which was very large" (16:4). Matthew describes it as "a great stone" (27:60). In order to understand the wonder of that stone's removal, it is important to know something about first-century burial customs and rock-hewn tombs.[3]

In Second Temple Judaism "to be buried in Jerusalem was considered a privilege because it was the Holy City, where the *Shekinah,* the 'radiant presence,' of the Lord resided."[4] The dark flip side of the cultural coin was that the Romans routinely refused burial to executed criminals. Leaving the rotting corpses of criminals crucified (often at heavily trafficked crossroads) was a powerful deterrent. For a Jew to be left unburied was considered an abomination (see Deut 28:26; Jer 8:1-3; and Ezek 29:5). So at some danger to himself, "good and righteous" Joseph of Arimathea appealed to Pilate for and was granted the body of Jesus (see

3. For more on the burial of Jesus and first-century tombs, see Joel B. Green, "Burial of Jesus," in *Dictionary of Jesus and the Gospels*, ed. Joel B. Green, Scott McKnight, and I. Howard Marshall (Downers Grove, IL: InterVarsity Press, 1992), 88–92; John J. Rousseau and Rami Arav, "Jerusalem, Tombs," in Rousseau and Arav, *Jesus and His World: An Archaeological and Cultural Dictionary* (Minneapolis: Fortress Press, 1995), 164–69; John Wilkinson, *The Jerusalem Jesus Knew* (Nashville, TN: Thomas Nelson Publishers, 1978), 155–159.

4. Rosseau and Arav, "Jerusalem, Tombs," 166.

Luke 23:51-53). Where the tomb he provided was located was for many years a matter of debate among archaeologists. It was almost certainly a rock-hewn, rolling-stone tomb, not only because the gospels describe it as such but because the "rocky ground in the Jerusalem area makes grave-digging difficult," and it was "desirable to forestall any possible delays."[5] By recounting that Pilate dispatched guards to the tomb who "made the tomb secure by sealing the stone" (Matt 27:66),[6] Matthew stresses the importance of the tomb as a proof of death.

Archaeology attests that burial practices in first-century Jerusalem and environs involved placing a body on a stone shelf in a natural cave or a tomb carved out of rock, leaving it there until the flesh had decayed and finally returning for the desiccated bones that were placed permanently in an ossuary, a stone box with a lid. Rock-hewn tombs had a small entrance, which was closed either with a square block of stone that functioned as a plug or with a rounded stone that could be rolled that was placed in a groove in front of the entrance. The stone was mainly to keep wild animals from entering but would also deter grave robbers

5. Wilkinson, *The Jerusalem Jesus Knew*, 156.

6. This requires the Matthean addition of 28:2-4 and 11-15, in which the guards who "became like dead men" when "an angel of the Lord . . . came and rolled back the stone" were subsequently bribed to tell an alternative version of events, that "his disciples came by night and stole him away."

and the "body snatchers" alluded to in Matthew's gospel. In either case, it would have been no easy task to move the stone. Mark's gospel reports that the spice-bearing women who went to Jesus' tomb "had been saying to one another, 'Who will roll away the stone for us from the entrance to the tomb?'" (16:3). It was apparently too heavy for three adult women to budge. But "when they looked up, they saw that the stone, which was very large, had already been rolled back" (Mark 16:4).[7]

The first function of our dual-purpose stone is to mark a genuine death. It is the impediment that keeps the women from accomplishing their purpose, which was to anoint a corpse. Life is like this. We have good intentions to do noble deeds, or just ordinary kindnesses, and the accomplishment of our aspiration is blocked. Metaphorically, there is a stone across the entrance way. Sometimes the stone is placed there by circumstances beyond our control—for example, by the systemic racism of which some of us are finally becoming aware. Or perhaps the "death stone" is placed by someone else, someone in authority over us. Sometimes, if we are honest, we admit that we have put it there ourselves, that *we block our own progress* toward our goals. We climb into our self-made tomb and block the opening with a stone *from the inside*. The good news is that if we put it there, we

7. In John's gospel, as well, Mary Magdalene has a similar experience when she "came to the tomb and saw the stone had been removed from the tomb" (John 20:1).

can remove it. The *better* news is that sometimes, like the women, when we *look up*, we see that the stone *has been rolled back* (Mark 16:4); we, like Jesus, *have been* resurrected. Passive voice. It was done to us or for us.

The heart of Christianity's message is that something with eternal consequences has been done for us that we could not do for ourselves. Mysteriously, and for our benefit, the stone of death, the stone that blocked entrance to what we sought or to our freedom, is removed. Matthew records that "an angel of the Lord, descending from heaven, came and rolled back the stone and sat on it" (28:2). What or who are the "angels" who have rolled back your "stones"? The stone that "kept you out" or "kept you in" or "blocked your way" has become a place for an angel to sit! The stone of death becomes the stone of possibility and new life.

The Stone of Resurrection

"They found the stone rolled away from the tomb" (Luke 24:2).

With varying degrees of specificity, all four gospels declare the stone had been rolled away or been moved and that Jesus had risen from the tomb:

> "[Y]ou are looking for Jesus of Nazareth, who was crucified. He has been raised; he is not here. Look, there is the place they laid him." (Mark 16:6)

"He is not here; for he has been raised. . . . Come, see the place where he lay." (Matt 28:6)

"Why do you look for the living among the dead? He is not here but has risen." (Luke 24:5)

Mary Magdalene came to the tomb and saw that the stone had been removed from the tomb. (John 20:1)

The stone that was intended to imprison, to be the proof and seal of death, has itself become the testimony to life. In all four gospels, the stone's movement is described in the passive voice. Something or someone moved it, and witnesses saw "the truth of the matter." Visible evidence was given of Jesus' resurrection, and that evidence began with the fact that the stone had been moved from the entrance to the tomb.

Actually it is the women who saw the stone placed over the tomb entrance. "The women who had come with him from Galilee . . . saw the tomb and how his body was laid" (Luke 23:55) and "found the stone rolled away from the tomb" (Luke 24:2).[8] It is not an insignificant detail of the narrative that Jesus' women disciples provide the continuity in the death/resurrection account. Luke Timothy Johnson's commentary on Luke notes that "Luke emphasizes the

---

8. Cf. Matt 27:60-61; 28:1-2 and Mark 15:47; 16:1-4, both of which explicitly say the women saw the tomb and burial and, the next day, experienced the stone's removal.

fidelity and function of the women from Galilee. . . . They provide the essential 'chain of evidence' for the Christian claims about Jesus."[9]

This fact is an indication of the importance of women in the new family or community or kingdom that Jesus announced. Johnson notes that "Luke emphasizes the role of the women as eyewitnesses."[10] When the man "in dazzling clothes" asks them to remember what Jesus told them in Galilee (Luke 24:4, 6), "they could remember because they had been there."[11] Those whose testimony might not be accepted in a contemporary court were entrusted with the eyewitness evidence of emerging Christianity's most important (and perhaps outrageous) claim and proclamation. But it is noteworthy that Mark's gospel suggests that they must "look up" (embrace a wider perspective than that of their own grief) to "see" (to comprehend or understand) this unexpected and astonishing fact.

Just as in an earlier chapter we noted that one would not expect a stone to speak, one would not expect a large one to move of its own volition. But it did move. However it happened, the stone's movement is the confirmation of risen life. The death stone becomes the resurrection stone.

9. Luke Timothy Johnson, *The Gospel of Luke*, Sacra Pagina (Collegeville, MN: Liturgical Press, 1991), 383.

10. Johnson, *The Gospel of Luke*, 391.

11. Johnson, *The Gospel of Luke*, 391. And see Luke 8:1-3, and Mark 16:40-41.

The great paradox is that the same stone that sealed a death also opened to life—and not just for Jesus, "the first fruits of those who have died" (1 Cor 15:20). One doesn't speak of the "first" unless others are expected to follow.

Concluding Reflections

Although I happen to believe it, this chapter is not intended to argue for the veracity of Jesus' resurrection. The stone in the story, and in all the texts we've examined, is, of course, both literal and a metaphor suggestive of spiritual truths. We could speculate about *how* the stone moved (*pace* Matthew) or take the narrative at face value as Luke and the other evangelists record it. The point for our discussion is that the "seal of death" became the doorway to Life, to the light the darkness cannot overcome (see John 1:5). St. John's gospel opens with the "punch line": "What has come into being in him [the Logos, Jesus] was life, and the life was the light of all people" (1:5). John's Jesus states clearly, "I came that they may have life" (10:10) and later reveals to Martha, "I am the resurrection and the life. Those who believe in me, even though they die, will live" (John 11:25; see also John 5:21-29).

This last paradigmatic stone, the one at Jesus' tomb, reminds us that life's impediments are like this: a lot depends upon when and how we "see" them. As in the resurrection narratives, sometimes the passage of time is required to understand the changing purpose or function of a "stone" in the larger story. To allude again to the scriptural metaphor beloved of 1 Peter, it takes time and reflection to understand how the "stone that the builders rejected" (or martyred) becomes "precious" and "the very head of the corner," the Christ of Christian faith.[12]

In a reflection in the devotional publication *Give Us This Day*, Judith Valente writes, "So often in Scripture we see objects such as stones become symbols for something deeper." She continues, "It is as if we need something we can see and hold to serve as touchstones, returning us again and again to what really matters."[13]

In a very real sense, the last stone of the last week is such a touchstone. Originally a touchstone was a black stone (usually related to flint) used to test the purity of gold or silver. If the ore or metal were genuine, when rubbed against the touchstone, it left a streak. Touchstones are tests of the genuineness of something, revealing its fundamental or quintessential feature. The mark that we leave when we rub against this last, paradoxically dual-purpose stone reveals as much about us as it does about Jesus' resurrection, about life from death, about death and life as two sides of the same "stone."

At the end of the book of Joshua (a book of which I am not overly fond), Joshua took "a large stone, and set it up there under the oak in the sanctuary of the Lord"

---

12. 1 Pet 2:6-8, quoting Ps 118:22 and Isa 8:14-15.

13. Judith Valente, "Touchstones," in *Give Us This Day* 7, no. 8 (August 2017): 202.

(24:26). At this point in her history, it is Israel's quintessential touchstone. "See," says Joshua "this stone shall be a witness against us; for it has heard all the words of the LORD that he spoke to us; therefore it shall be a witness against you, if you deal falsely with your God. So Joshua sent the people away to their inheritances" (24:27-28). Judge Joshua doesn't judge. He sets up a stone before the people, and then the stone judges. In Luke's gospel, the women "found the stone rolled away from the tomb" (24:2). The stone that sealed Jesus' death no longer covered the entrance to his tomb. Like Joshua's stone, it became a witness. And like Joshua's stone, it remains a judge. Of us.

I began these meditations with a poem about stones, and I shall close it with one.

"The Stone"
(Mark 16:3-4)

The Myrrhbearers came
(with what fear and trembling?)
trudging along in darkness
worrying about
the stone.

Everybody worries about
the stone,
that great impediment
between us
and what we seek,

that great burden
we carry
like Sisyphus
laboring
up and down the hill.

The sun rose.
The women looked up.
The stone,
which was very large,
had been removed.

No wonder they ran
to tell Cephas.
Somebody should tell Sisyphus:
"Put it down, man,
and dance on it."[14]

14. Bonnie Thurston, "The Stone," in Thurston, *Practicing Silence: New and Selected Verses* (Brewster, MA: Paraclete, 2014), 60.

Rolling Back the Stone

"The Lord spoke to Moses, saying . . . command the rock before their eyes to yield its water. Thus you shall bring water out of the rock for them." (Numbers 20:7-8)

The epilogue of a book is usually a conclusion that summarizes the message, the "point" of the previous material. It "closes the door" on the book. This epilogue is intended to open the door a bit wider, to help the reader see beyond the specific stones of the last week of Jesus' life, what they suggest, and glimpse wider implications of instances of the biblical metaphor of stones or rocks. I am not suggesting that "rocks aren't rocks," that the narratives in which they occur aren't historical, but that biblical rocks might be "more than rocks."

Generally speaking, rocks get a "bad rap." Years ago when I taught at a Jesuit college, a male colleague from another part of the United States kindly came to rototill my West

Virginia garden and subsequently declared unappreciatively, "I've never been any place with so many rocks in the soil." Rocks are a nuisance, but they also leach nutrients into the soil, and, as a gardener knows, they aerate it. Another negative example is the proverb, "You can't get blood from a stone." Stones are dead, inert. Don't expect anything life-giving from them. Perhaps more germane to this book, rocks are considered impediments. They get in the way. There are, however, other ways to view stones. I hope this short study has made clear that the stones in the last week of Jesus' life are not just impediments but invite us to "rehabilitate" our attitude toward rocks, and other things, as well.

If you have persevered this far, you know this book is, in part, an exercise in imagination and, exegetically, a lifting up of Scripture's multivalency, the many meanings and many levels of meaning of the texts. I am not alone in this approach. The great Alexandrian rabbis distinguished at least four separate but complimentary meanings in Scripture: the literal, historical sense (*peshat*); the hidden sense of the Mosaic law (*remez*); the allegorical sense (*daruish*); and the mystical sense (*sod*). Alexandrian Christian theologians and exegetes, the most famous of whom is probably Origen (ca. 185–254), essentially agreed with the rabbis. Origen believed that every passage and word of Scripture bore spiritual meaning. The book you have read is a modern example of Alexandrian interpretation.

Much of Scripture is like poetry, in that it uses one thing to illuminate something else. Of course, Jesus does this when he says, "The kingdom of heaven is like. . . ." His parables operate on this principle. The word *parable* literally means "throw (*ballo*) beside (*para*)." Jesus the teacher challenges us to see things differently, to look more deeply, to remember that things might not be as they appear. A Samaritan might be the hero of the story. The impoverished widow might give more than the wealthy. The sinner who knows he is one might be the "good guy," and the righteous person might slink away sad.

There are many examples of both the positive and the negative metaphorical use of stones and rocks in the gospels. It is remarkable how many times in Hebrew Scripture God is the rock. "The LORD is my rock, my fortress, and my deliverer, / my God, my rock in whom I take refuge," declares Psalm 18:2, a psalm of David (and see Pss 19:14 and 92:15). I am reminded of the Negro spiritual: "My God is a rock in a weary land . . . a shelter in the time of storm." Isaiah suggests, "[I]n the LORD GOD / you have an everlasting rock" (26:4) and reminds his hearers, "Look to the rock from which you were hewn" (51:1). A good concordance will provide many other examples.

Rocks appear in many ways in the New Testament with both positive and negative connotations. John the Baptist suggests, "God is able from these stones to raise up children to Abraham" (Matt 3:9). Perhaps with Psalms in mind, Matthew's Jesus closes the Sermon on the Mount by comparing those who hear and do his word with a wise man who built his house upon a rock (7:24-27). When asked, during his entry into Jerusalem, to quiet the noisy, joyful crowd, Jesus responds, "[I]f these were silent, the stones would shout out" (Luke 19:40). We have already examined Jesus' quotation of Psalm 118:22: "The stone that the builders rejected / has become the chief cornerstone." The image of the rejected stone stands behind 1 Peter 2:1-8, with a remarkable twist. The author of 1 Peter applies the quotation from the psalm to Jesus, himself, inviting the letter's recipients to "come to him, a living stone" and "like living stones, let yourselves be built into a spiritual house" (1 Pet 2:4-5). This may be the ultimate "rehabilitation" of stones. It certainly links the Hebrew Bible's image of God as rock with the person of Jesus.

Biblical rocks, and especially the stones of the last week of Jesus' earthly life, invite us to do as the writer of 1 Peter did, to see things differently, perhaps to see good where there appears to be none. Geologically, if you know which rocks to crack open, you will find amazing crystals or gems. But you have to break the rock. Spiritually, I am reminded of the three visionary experiences of the English Catholic spiritual writer Caryll Houselander in which she saw the face of Jesus in unlikely people and places. And that is because she *looked*.[1]

There are any number of biblical examples of good things from unlikely places. For example, in obedience to

1. See Houselander's autobiography, *A Rocking Horse Catholic* (New York: Sheed and Ward, 1955). Wendy M. Wright's *Caryll Houselander: Essential Writings* (Maryknoll, NY: Orbis, 2005) is an excellent introduction to her life and writing.

God, Moses does what others think impossible: he brings water from a rock—and not just a trickle but enough for all the people *and* all their livestock (Num 20:2-13). Fisherman Simon the blusterer and waverer becomes Peter (*Petrus*), the rock on whose confession the church is built (Matt 16:17-19). Jesus saw something in him other than that he was "dense." The very large rock that covered the opening of Jesus' tomb, the image of his death, when moved, becomes the doorway to his (and our) resurrection. Sometimes the value of a big stone is in moving it slightly.

Stones can be valuable for what is in them, what arises from them, and what lies behind them. It is easy to forget that when I stub my physical or spiritual toe on a stone or when a big rock seems to block my movement. It is precisely then that I am invited to see the stone differently. Paradigmatically, the big stone at Jesus' tomb becomes the way to his resurrection. The biggest impediments, obstacles, and barriers *might* be something very different indeed. But they won't "change" or offer alternatives if I don't take up the challenge of thinking differently about them, if I don't remember to live into the multivalency of Holy Scripture and its invitation to see things from multiple angles and, therefore, differently. I hope this brief exposition of the stones of the last week of Jesus has invited the reader to do just this and given some examples of how to do it.

In his poem "In Silence," which explores human identity and its "environs," American Trappist monk and spiritual writer Thomas Merton invites us to listen precisely where we might not expect to hear anything, to listen to a *stone* wall. Merton may have had in mind part of a verse from the prophet Habakkuk· "The very stones will cry out from the wall" (Hab 2:11). In any case, the invitation to "hear differently" is also a reminder to "see differently," a reminder that things like stones might be more, might contain more, than they appear to do. Here are the first lines of Merton's poem:

Be still
Listen to the stones of the wall.
Be silent, they try
To speak your

Name.
Listen
To the living walls.[2]

Be still. Listen. Be silent. And you might hear a "dead thing" (a stone wall or a rock) speak to you. You might realize that what appears to be dead can be very much alive and that potentially *everything* is "speaking." And if you do so, you may become the "Moses" who sustains others by bringing water from the rock or the wise person who builds on a rock or the one who pushes the big stone from someone else's tomb.

2. Thomas Merton, "In Silence," in *The Collected Poems of Thomas Merton* (New York: New Directions, 1977), 280.